FORGED IN THE FIRES

The Seven Catalysts to Ignite your Possible, Accelerate Your Potential & Extricate Your Best

FIREMAN ROB

ABSOLUTE AUTHOR PUBLISHING HOUSE
NEW ORLEANS, LA

Absolute Author
Publishing House

Forged in the Fires
Copyright © 2019 by Fireman Rob.
All rights reserved.

Publisher: Absolute Author Publishing House, LLC
Editor: Dr. Melissa Caudle
Cover Designer: Angie Alaya
Illustrator: *Robert Verhelst*
Photographs*: From the private collection of Robert Verhelst*

IN-PUBLICATION-DATA LIBRARY OF CONGRESS

    p. cm.
        Fireman Rob/ *Forged in the Fires*

ISBN: 978-1-951028-36-7

    1.   Self-help 2. Mind and Body 3. Motivational Memoir

PRINTED IN THE UNITED STATES OF AMERICA

TABLE OF CONTENTS

FOREWORD

By Bonner Paddock

I first met Rob at the 2012 *Ironman World Championships* in Kailua-Kona, Hawaii. Two days before the race, we sat together on a panel of "special" athletes. Our select group intended to swim 2.4 miles, bike 112 miles, and run a full marathon differently from most of the other 2,000 competitors. We were doing "it" for something bigger than ourselves. Looking back at that afternoon on stage, I still get goosebumps. My fellow panelists came from all over the world, and we each shared our remarkable paths until this moment. Having been born with cerebral palsy, the race was set to be the most grueling challenge of my life, yet.

On the team of panelists was an athlete who had beaten cancer four times -- his survival necessitating over seventy-five surgeries. Another guy, who I considered a madman at the time, would attempt to do the marathon leg of the *Ironman* in one of the most humid places on the planet while burdened with over fifty pounds of fire gear. He was known simply by everyone as Fireman Rob.

As the panel came to an end, the master of ceremonies asked each athlete a final question, "What is your best guess on finishing time?"

One by one, the competitors announced a time many hours shy of the 17-hour cutoff time on the course. The whole time, knowing well my body's continuous fight against itself, I quietly wondered, "am I the only one who's going to say seventeen hours.

Then the madman, sitting just to my right, declared, "I am planning to just slip under the cutoff."

After the panel broke up, I had to meet this guy. He was even nuttier than me, and I had the sense that we were somehow bound together on this mission to finish the Kona Ironman. Surprisingly, Fireman Rob introduced himself with a big smile and a deep chuckle in his voice. He asked for a photograph with me, and we soon got talking. We discussed and shared ideas about our game plans for race day, our passion for helping people through actions, and the improbability of what we were attempting to do in Hawaii. Nobody had ever finished the Kona Ironman burdened with a fireman gear, and nobody had ever finished the race with cerebral palsy either. We were both attempting to break world records in our own right. From that first meeting, Fireman Rob and I became bound to each other like brothers.

On race day, we supported one another, beginning with the walk down together into the ocean at the start, all the way through to Mile 24 on the marathon -- with both of us struggling to finish before the 17-hour cutoff. Since near the halfway point of the running leg of the Ironman, I had been slowly gaining on Rob, and I mean, slowly. Ahead, I could see his reflectors on his fire suit sleeves and pants in the pitch of the night. They were almost like a beacon that I was drawn to meet. Then a couple of miles from the finish, those reflectors looked to have stopped moving. At this point, I was in bad shape. My body was shutting down. My legs had become lead heavy and I often felt like I was hallucinating, so I couldn't trust my eyes. Maybe Rob was still moving, and I wasn't. That was entirely possible.

As I continued onward, however, I came upon Rob. He was on his knees, buckled over in agony. He was clearly struggling to continue. I wanted to help, but if I stopped even for a moment, I knew I would collapse. Still, I hesitated beside him and asked if he was okay. I wanted to make sure he was not tapping out. He extended his arm, laden with the weight of his fire suit, and gave me a thumbs up. I patted him on the back and said, "We both may die at the finish line."

We laughed and then I pushed myself forward, onward, sure he would make it there. We did not see each other again until the medical tent where a crowd of doctors and attendants fed us IV drips and covered our bodies in reflective heat blankets. We had done it though. We had each claimed our world records.

Over the years, our paths have crossed many times and our bond has deepened, as has my admiration for Rob and the impact he is making in the world.

I could not be more honored he asked me to introduce his book to readers. Rob walks the talk. He is an individual of profound passion and iron will. He takes ownership of the hard choices and pursues great challenges with resilience and supreme calm. For those of you who choose to learn the Seven Catalysts and implement them into your daily life, I am confident that they will elevate your happiness, success, well-being, and love for life.

PREFACE

The story of becoming Fireman Rob was forged in fires of my life, creating catalysts to move forward in my life while paying it forward through racing for a purpose, and speaking to help others find their life.

DEDICATION

MY MOM & DAD

In my life, I have been blessed with parents who have loved me, believed in me and supported me through my wonderful moments and rough growing moments. My mom and dad are my true North and have made me the person I am today. I continue to grow and build who I am throughout my journey of life. Mom and Dad, Dad who is looking down on me from above, you have shown me that it is okay to cry when hurting, smile when happy, and love when feeling loved. Most of all you have shown me how to be the best version of myself.

I love you both so much for everything you have given me and for showing me the truest meaning of unconditional love.

MY FAMILY

My loving wife and best friend, Nicole, who has been my rock in healing and my life's true love. You make me the best person I can be and show me love in so many ways, from helping me discover what being content is to enjoying being together & still. I love you, and I am so blessed to have found my true love.

My kids, Noah, Payton, and Avery, seeing you during races makes me want to keep pushing to find the best me. You make me smile and prove to me every day that life is wonderful. Your joy, your compassion and just being yourselves makes me so truly happy. Life is wonderful because of you.

FORGED IN THE FIRES

IGNITION

This is your life, your one-and-only life.

IGNITION

Our lives depend on strength to thrive; otherwise, we struggle to find success in life. I created this book to offer my catalysts and help you find and live your potential. Life isn't easy, and discovering your true self takes courage. I can't give you that, but I will give you catalysts I learned forging my life's strength in fire. Enjoy and thrive. Life doesn't get easier; you get stronger.

Chapter 1

ABOUT FIREMAN ROB

Success is not a goal; it is a byproduct of
a journey down the right path.

Chapter 1:

ABOUT FIREMAN ROB

My name is Robert Verhelst, yet most people know me as Fireman Rob. I am a career firefighter for the City of Madison, Wisconsin since 2000, an Air Force veteran, and did search and recovery at the World Trade Center after the September 11th Attacks.

My mission to inspire people to "Live your passion" started in 2011 when I did *Ironman Wisconsin*, which landed on the 10th anniversary of 9/11. I did it differently than most, though, and to honor those who lost their lives and those who responded, I did the 2.4-mile swim, 112-mile bike, and then donned my full firefighter gear (helmet, bunker pants, jacket, and air pack weighing 50 lbs.) for the 26.2-mile run. I finished the race in 16 hours and 17 minutes, igniting an insatiable drive to inspire others to find their passions and LIVE!

Since that moment in 2011, I have completed twenty-three *Ironman* distance and twenty-eight half *Ironman* distance triathlons in full firefighter gear for every run portion. In 2015, I pushed the envelope of what is possible and broke the Guinness World Record for the *Most Ironman* 70.3 Triathlons in one year with twenty-three. The existing record had been done in normal triathlon gear, but I broke it by completing each run portion in my fire gear. There was no extra-record nor credit for the fire gear, but the purpose for it was to ignite the globe to understand what we are capable of when driven by passion.

In addition, I started the Fireman Rob Foundation in 2013, and since that date, we have delivered 7,000 Gund Teddy Bears to children in hospitals throughout the world. Our mission is simply to #BearASMILE on children in need of a moment of happiness. SMILE to me means (Simple Moments Impact Lives Every day).

My life has been a training ground for understanding and developing my message of the power that mental strength brings to a motivated, passion-driven life. My action-based experiences through firefighting and endurance athletics, my time at Ground Zero in NY (09-11-01), and my philanthropy have enabled me to become a leading voice for personal growth or empowerment. I deliver an empowering message to an audience about engaging their passion, through mental strength, to live to their true potential. Our lives depend on strength to thrive; otherwise, we struggle to find success in life.

Action always beats intention, and I continue to challenge and grow through my life's journey.

BASICS:

- Hometown: Madison, Wisconsin, USA
- Husband & Father of 3
- Career Firefighter for City of Madison, Wisconsin, USA since 2000
- Collegiate Basketball & Water Polo player
- Professional Motivational / Inspirational Keynote Speaker
- Professional Corporate & Group Trainer in Leadership & Mental Performance
- Founder/COO of Fireman Rob Foundation
- Certified Ironman University Coach

LIFE EXPERIENCES:

- Sponsored Endurance Athlete (wearing full firefighter gear)
- 9/11 Rescue Worker
- Air Force Veteran
- Bachelor of Science in Resource Management (Troy University)
- Master of Science in Emergency Management (Columbia Southern University)
- PTSD Survivor

ACCOLADES:

- United States Air Force
  - Air Force Achievement Medal
  - 325th Medical Group Airman of the Quarter
- 2012 Ironman Performance of the Year
- 2012 HITS Triathlon Athlete of the Year
- 2014 In Business Magazine "25 Most Influential People in Greater Madison"
- 2015 Jefferson Award
- 2015 Triathlon Magazine "Best Record-Breaking Performance of the Year"
- Guinness World Record for Most Ironman 70.3 Triathlons in One Year in 2015 (23 in firefighter gear for run portions)
- 2015 Globe Turnout Feet of Strength (Athleticism category)
- World Record for Most *Ironman* triathlons in Full Firefighter Gear
- World Record for Most Half *Ironman* Triathlons in Full Firefighter Gear
- Selected member of The National Society of Leadership and Success (CSU)
- Founded the Fireman Rob Foundation in 2013 (www.FiremanRobFoundation.com)
  - *Mission:* "Spreading our passion of being part of something bigger, one bear at a time, delivering smiles to disadvantaged children & children in hospitals throughout the world."
  - Delivered over 7,000 bears all over the world

Chapter 2

THE 7 CATALYSTS

The whole is greater than the sum of its parts.

Chapter 2:

THE SEVEN CATALYSTS

I have found that throughout my far-from-linear life, I was able to continue to move one step forward, even in darkness and confusion, by using these seven catalysts. Now, I want you to know that I did not create these, nor are they magic. I just took the time to look backward, forward, and in the present at myself and my surroundings, while asking, "What are the catalysts that drive me to live daily and why?"

Will this book and the seven catalysts change your life or maybe a part of it? That will be up to you and how you apply them to your life. You will need to put the words to actions and actions to habits to make a change. I hope you read this book and drive forward into your life of opportunity and LIVE WITH PASSION. It is what you are meant to do.

The seven catalysts tie together like this.

Our lives demand purpose or passion for moving forward with motivation and desire to live. Once we **find purpose**, then we can find the strength to **take ownership** of our actions, in-actions, words and habits. This is so important because it will create a strength in us to be able to **make decisions** without fear of success or failure. Deciding to act is key, since understanding our path will lead us to be more emotionally in control when faced with adversity or fear. When we **control our emotions** through the darkness, we can **build resilience** by stepping outside our comfort zones to find our true potential. This resilience along with our purpose will drive us to **have** more **faith** in ourselves and less fear of the unknown. With a piece of these six catalysts, we build our **mental strength** which, I believe, is our greatest asset in finding ourselves and living our potential forged in the fires. My dad would always say, "You can't control what someone else does, just control what you do." We must try in our lives to be not a person of success, but rather a person of value.

Chapter 3

1ST CATALYST

PASSION

Be authentic, no matter what, everything starts with purpose.

Chapter 3:

PASSION – 1ST CATALYST

Passion: It is our why. It is our strength. Passion is our focus in life. It is something that is there when challenges or obstacles seem too much to bear. It is that extra gear or newfound energy that prods us on when most would quit. Why would we not want to find out what it is for ourselves? Are we afraid we cannot truly live it or, perhaps, have we never even thought about it? Are we merely surviving?

In the fire service, there is something we term "Backdraft." It is a dramatic explosive event during a fire, resulting from the rapid re-introduction of oxygen into an oxygen-depleted environment to elicit combustion. An example would be breaking a window or opening the door to an enclosed space where the fire was dormant due to lack of oxygen, with the fire just waiting to rear its ugly head. Backdrafts present a serious threat to firefighters and are not something desirable, but the correlation often made between passion and fire is relevant.

How many of us have reached the point where we ask ourselves, "Is this all life has for me?" or "Is this the best I can be?" This is life in a passion-depleted environment. There is no FIRE! Yet, if we take the time and have the courage to introduce passion into that environment, bearing in mind the risk, we will explosively ignite the life we should have. We can't fear it; we must understand it and use it to our advantage. The courage of firefighters is forged in the fires, and so must passion.

We can look at passion as a talent. Everyone has some level of passion, but not everyone is brave enough to create the opportunity to embrace this talent. To survive, most of us prefer to be practical rather than passionate. We must be brave enough to acknowledge and embrace our passion, and thus realize that is where our strength is.

"In order to survive, most of us prefer to be practical rather than passionate."

Practical keeps us in the comfort zone. Yes, it can be scary to push outside that zone; however, passion means ignoring the comfort zone and finding our truest potential. It means seeking our own success and not what someone else might define as success. What makes us passionate is what drives us to be who we are destined to be, not what others see us as being.

In 2015, I decided to break the Guinness World Record for the most 70.3 triathlons in one year. The record at the time was twenty-two. While the holder of this record had done the races more conventionally, I decided to forego the spandex triathlon gear customarily worn for the half marathon portion of the race and don my full firefighter gear instead. This meant an extra fifty pounds of firefighter jacket, bunker pants, air pack and fire helmet (running shoes, not boots). I was not focused on merely setting a record; my mission was my passion to inspire others through my actions.

CERTIFICATE

The most Ironman 70.3 races completed in a year is 23 and was accomplished by Robert Verhelst (USA) of Waunakee, Wisconsin, USA, between 10 January and 8 November 2015.

I had set out to do twenty-six half *Ironman* distance triathlons in a year, but by the end of the year, I was unable to meet that goal. I finished the year still breaking the world record, but only by one race. Throughout the long, arduous journey of this world record year, I found out that there was so much more to reach for goals that no one else had previously accomplished. I had to make a path, both physically and mentally, but I had no direction, no understanding of the journey, and no solid, definitive way to finish. Realistically, there was no way I should have been able to do this.

There were moments throughout the journey when I felt lost. Moments when I didn't have a way to finish what I had set out to do. Yet, beyond all the seeming impossibilities that lurked in my mind, there was the passion that drove me to show myself and my children what a passionate soul can accomplish. I am often asked what it is like to hold a Guinness World Record. I am happy that I accomplished my goal, but the record is simply a piece of paper that needs periodic dusting. It is the journey that is valuable, that has lasting significance.

ACTION

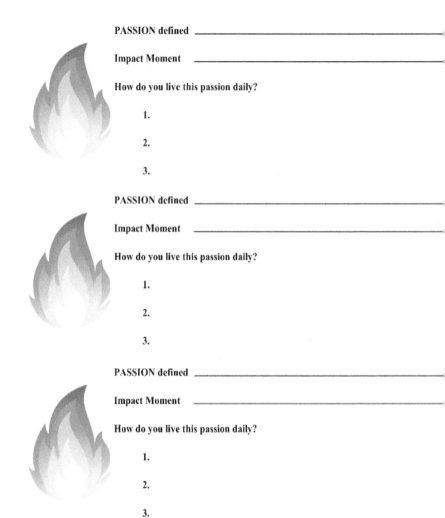

PASSION defined _____

Impact Moment _____

How do you live this passion daily?

1.

2.

3.

PASSION defined _____

Impact Moment _____

How do you live this passion daily?

1.

2.

3.

PASSION defined _____

Impact Moment _____

How do you live this passion daily?

1.

2.

3.

"The hardest person you will ever have
to lead is yourself."

– BILL GEORGE

The word passion derives from a Latin word meaning "to suffer." How does suffering equate with passion? Well, because it is about perseverance, a willingness to suffer to endure. Passion gives meaning to "why," often coming from impact moments in our lives that tell us what we are willing to fight for. Finding our passion isn't easy; it is having a conversation with ourselves, finding why we go forward and persevere, and how we ignite our actions with fire that sustains our perseverance. Sometimes, an event in our lives has an impact that lets us see our own passion and find a new path into the future. Following your passion is having the courage to lead yourself to your true potential.

So, it is that I found a passion of mine on September 11, 2011, when I did *Ironman Wisconsin*. This was my first full *Ironman* in firefighter gear for the run. I was doing it to remember those from 9/11 who had lost their lives. At the *Ironman* banquet, I was asked to give a little speech about what I was doing and why I was doing it. I had no idea what I would say. I had written out something, but once I got up on the stage, I didn't need to read it. My passion brought out the words. I was about to do something that no one else had ever done, knowing there would be physical and mental struggles to overcome, but as I spoke, I could feel the strength of my passion. Not only was I passionate about what I was going to do in the race, but I was also discovering my passion for sharing the story of my journey. Looking at the audience, the emotion on their faces empowered me, giving me the strength, I needed to share my story.

This speech transitioned into the first prepared speech I would give in New York City for Timex Company. Having no formal training as a speaker, I worked on a PowerPoint and thought I had crafted a great speech. Yet again, my crafted speech would give way to the message the strength of my passion wanted to deliver. My heart was speaking about the struggles, experiences, and lessons forged in the fires, my fires.

That first speech gave me a power I had not felt post 9/11. I needed to share what I felt, and, to this day, I continue to have the passion I found on September 11, 2011, when I was given the opportunity to speak to all the *Ironman* athletes. I have come to understand my passion for offering perspective to others, for sharing my story and helping others find their true passion so that they can forge their strength in their life's fires.

ACTION

Fears or Facts

What scares you from following your passion? What hurdles do you see? Mental or Physical?

What FEARS do you see in the distance or live with?

_____   _____

_____   _____

_____   _____

What Mental obstacles do you have?

_____

_____

_____

_____

_____

To overcome, you must first identify what kind of fear or obstacle it is, then move forward.

"It's not true that passion is something that you have to feel or touch in the physical form, sometimes it is an effect of what you do. It is the outcome and impact of your journey on you and others."

Sometimes, the most poignant part of my passion is its effect on others. Our journey living our passion will almost always impact someone else. While it isn't something that can be touched or felt in physical form, passion is felt intensely by those who witness its enactment. Our words are the start, but our actions are evidence of the power within our passion that translates to others in a personal way. Our personal journey with our own passion is ours to nurture or destroy. The effect our passion has on others can be far-reaching and develop a life of its own in another person.

In 2011, on the tenth anniversary of 9/11, I set out to do *Ironman Wisconsin* in full firefighter turnout gear for the 26.2-mile run portion of the race. Due to reasons I honestly didn't fully understand at that time, I felt compelled to do something impactful. One that would honor the courage and sacrifice of those firefighters who had lost their lives on that day. This was a new idea, and the challenges were daunting.

The swim didn't bother me at all; I could swim 2.4 miles and found I was energized as I went out on the bike to travel 112 miles through the rolling, brutal hills around Madison. The bike has taken a little longer than usual. I need to be diligent on the walk. My mind must switch quickly from the pain and anguish of the bike to the challenge of a marathon in my full firefighter gear. No excuses just perform.

It's interesting how the pain changes throughout the race. I pushed the pain of the bike ride out of my mind, knowing that there will be a new kind of pain coming up. I needed to regroup as I go to change into my gear. I donned my fire gear. Every clap, high five and cheer along the way moved me forward. I realized this was going to be something special. The 26.2-mile journey to the finish was compelling, with stories throughout, emotional reactions, support from my brothers and sisters each time I passed the fire station, encouragement and heartwarming responses from spectators. This was my passion in action, igniting a sense of something greater than just this race.

Crossing the finish line with my hands held high, every part of my body yelled at me in pain. The music and deafening cheers from the crowd banging on the sides of the chute resounded in my head. I knew they felt the power of that finish line and my passion and struggle over 16 hours of pain. It was all worth it.

ACTION

Passion into Action Formula

Action you will do to achieve this?

Understand It	

Find out what your passion is and why you have it?

Write It	

Write down your passion and your why, then show it to valued support. Accountabili

Map It	

Make a plan that has daily goals, short term goals and the end goal.

Live It	

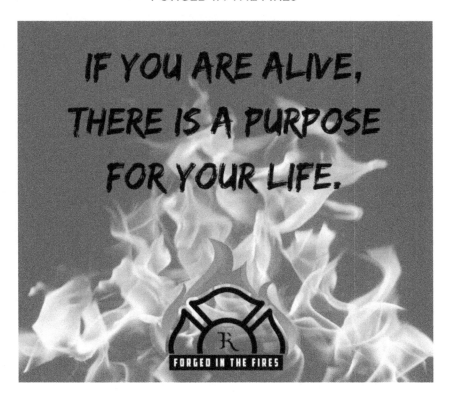

Chapter 4

OWNERSHIP

Choose your paths in life. They won't always be straight but trust in the journey.

Chapter 4:

OWNERSHIP – 2ND CATALYST

One of the least salient aspects of most people's lives is taking ownership of every decision and choice. We tend to make excuses for why we didn't get to the finish or why we live the way we do. We settle for being a lesser version of ourselves because we don't want the blame that owning our actions or words may entail.

Personally, ownership is about accepting and being accountable for my actions and beliefs. My life is comprised of conscious choices that I must own to move forward. One way you can build emotional resilience is to own what's happening to you instead of running away to seek comfort. The power of taking ownership for every action, decision, or goal brings you to a greater understanding of who you are and makes you align everything to your purpose or passion.

Ownership is about accountability, and in the fire service, we use accountability through our incidents to track and maintain safety and operational effectiveness. This accountability is at the incident command level; yet, the accountability, at the firefighter level, deals directly with life or death. Each person is accountable for his/her actions on a scene, where one wrong action could lead to death. This is not what most people have to go through daily, but it is the ultimate ownership situation. Our daily ownership decisions are important as well, although with mitigated adverse outcomes. In the fire service, there is an action called "bailout." This is reserved as a last-ditch survival option, but never as a first option. In our daily lives, bailing out should never be the first option either. Our purpose drives our ownership of our skills, thoughts and actions. Win, lose, live or die, I choose my path.

Taking ownership is challenging and even though it can be heart-wrenching at times, it is always necessary. Running away from difficulties and seeking comfort in excuses pushes us backward and weakens us. Owning what is happening to us gives us strength and resilience to get through the bad times and follow our passions.

"Ownership is about you accepting you and being accountable for your actions and beliefs. Own your life if you want to."

A simple part of ownership is the awareness of circumstances, understanding the entirety of an occurrence, and making our actions and words something for which we can be held accountable. We all have opinions, but do we own what we say? Do we understand its significance and what it really means? Do our actions match our words?

My ownership requires understanding the full situation of which I am part. My choices depend on this understanding and my subsequent ownership as well. This became starkly evident to me a couple of years ago. My son loves hockey. When he started playing, I had no idea what he was experiencing since my history involved basketball, swimming, and water polo. While watching one of his practice sessions when he was eight, I noticed at the end of the hour and a half practice that his effort seemed to be waning. Prior to that, my refrain to him was that he should always give his full effort. Naturally, seeing him slowing and seemingly coasting bothered me. I asked him what happened, and he said, "Dad, it's hard. I'm tired."

So, I did what every level-headed parent would do by signing up for an old man's hockey league, appropriately named "The Old Buzzard's League." I went to Dick's Sporting Goods and bought $300-$400 worth of equipment for myself. I was going to play hockey for the first time, ever. I needed to know what I was talking about when I questioned Noah's effort.

Before the first game, I said to Noah, "Buddy, I'm nervous."

He replied, "All you have to do is give effort, Dad."

Of course, there were no practices before the first game since all the other people had played before and knew what they were doing. I got on the ice during warm-ups, feeling good. It was exhilarating coasting across the ice. After ten minutes of warm-ups, the game began. I was on the third line, obviously. The first task was to get over the boards and onto the ice during my shift, not an easy task with my equipment, size and lack of dexterity. Suddenly, I am in the middle of a hockey game. One second the puck was heading to the other end, and the next it was heading toward our end. I was desperately moving from one end to the other, chasing the elusive puck.

Fifteen seconds into the game, I think I may die. *This is crazy hard. How does Noah do this for an hour and a half without shift changes?* I survive to go home, text my Dad with a message to explain the reality of hockey and tell Noah how proud I am of his effort on the ice. I finally understood what he went through. My experience has given me perspective. This is an important part of ownership, understanding the full situation so that my words are based on accountability.

ACTION

<u>How do you own your actions? Why do you want to own them?</u>

Habits to OWN your Actions

Now	Future

"Ownership is about leading from the frontline and setting an example. You cannot lead where you do not go.

Ownership is about leading from the frontline and leading by example by being THE EXAMPLE. It's not believing the b**** and being humble to the mistakes. When I lead, I and others need to believe every word and action comes from positivity. If I lead, I am thought of as the person who has the drive to be successful and make others successful as well. As a firefighter, those who follow me into the fire have to believe that I will have them come out on the other side. I must own my decisions, whether they cause success, trauma, failure, or doubt. In a fire situation, I am always accountable and will lead with full ownership of my decisions, having the courage to make mistakes and learn from them. I will own my success as well as my failure, whether in the fire service or my life.

After basic training, I went to the backside of the Lackland Air Force base to go through USAF Pararescue Indoctrination Course. This was the first step in becoming special operations for the USAF as a PJ. We had all kinds of water confidence, physical challenges and mostly mental challenges.

One day, we went to a lake right outside of San Antonio.

To get there, we had to get up very early morning to reach the schoolhouse.

"DROP!"

We start pushing away the earth doing pushups while waiting for the yellow school buses to take us to the lake. As the buses pull up,

"Grab your rucks and onto the buses. Two to a seat. Let's move!!!!"

Onto the bus, we went. Destination? Water confidence and fins; or so we thought.

I'm exhausted, was the only thing going through my mind.

We pile out of the bus, and there's the not so beautiful lake. Brown, like the last class... well you know.

"Get your fins, weight belts, BC's, snorkel, masks, and meet me down in formation at the shore."

I tear into my ruck like it was a Christmas package, and pulled all the things out and placed my ruck in the line before hustling down to formation to find out what our next evolution would be.

"The evolution will be with a buddy. You and your buddy will rescue-swim across this lake..."

"Where the Hell is the other side of this lake?" someone asks.

We were to find out later that it was about a 3-mile swim. Now, the concept of 'buddy swims' was that we'd face our buddy through the whole swim while swimming on our side with one arm up and one arm at our side.

The cadre continues with the details of the evolution.

"When you finish your swim, I need you to make sure you empty the water from your fins. Let this evolution begin."

We jump into the water, and the swim goes great, albeit extremely exhausting. We reach the shore; I stand up in the water, take off my fins and start running out of the water to get in formation.

We kicked ass, there is only three other groups out of the water, was what was running through my mind when reality, quite literally, hit my chest in the form of my cadre's hands.

"Give me your fins," he barks as he grabs them from me.

And that's when I remember, just as the water starts hitting the ground from the fins.

"So, you are one of those who don't think they have to follow all the rules. Start pushing away my earth until everyone is in formation. NOW!"

Every challenge we did brought in physical fatigue and the need to use our mind to ensure we finish and finish correctly. There was a need to make us understand that fatigue cannot make you forget details that could save your life or complete your mission.

ACTION

<u>What mistakes have you made that felt catastrophic?</u>
<u>Do you hide or run into the fire?</u>

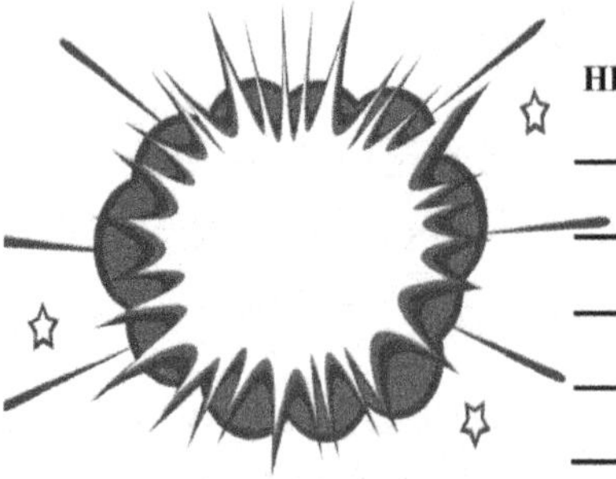

HIDE or RUN into the fire (Circle One and State Why)

_____

_____

_____

_____

_____

_____

What was the mistake?
Write in Explosion.

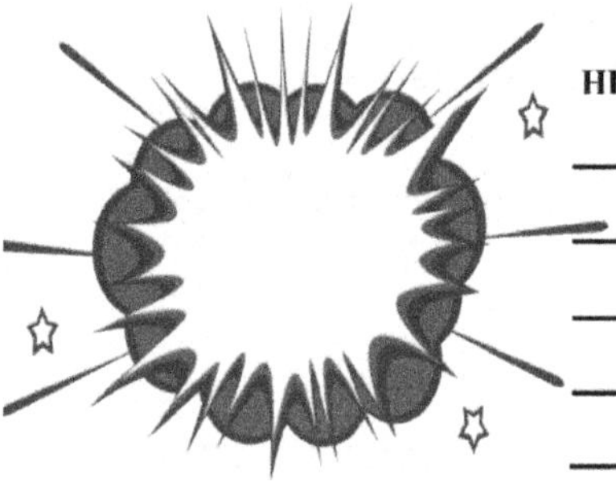

HIDE or RUN into the fire (Circle One and State Why)

_____

_____

_____

_____

_____

What was the mistake?
Write in Explosion.

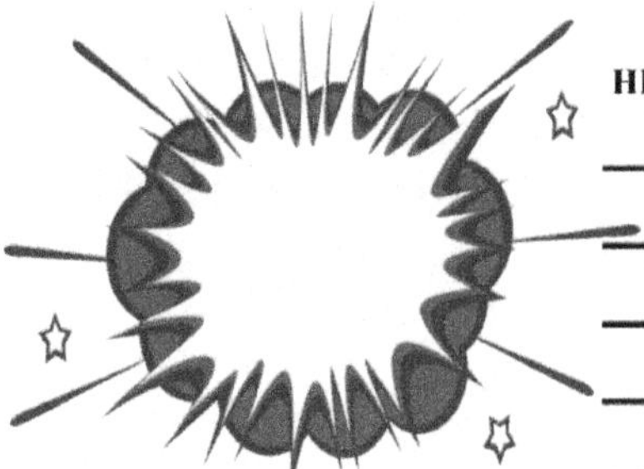

HIDE or RUN into the fire (Circle One and State Why)

_____

_____

_____

_____

_____

What was the mistake?
Write in Explosion.

"One of the least utilized aspects in most people's lives is taking ownership in every decision and choice they make. People are more apt to make excuses for why they didn't get to the finish or live like they do."

Sometimes, ownership of something in our lives is hidden in the form of denial. Taking ownership entails coming to terms with events and emotions that lead to a denial of what we need to own. Often, there are things we do to try to deal with the emotional trauma that doesn't really amount to healthy reactions. When we come to the realization that we have not dealt with the trauma, we begin to take ownership and find a healthy understanding of where we are.

In 2013, I ran a race in Mont Tremblant, Canada. It was a full *Ironman* distance race, and I did it in full firefighter gear for the run portion of the triathlon. The race went well, and the community was unbelievably supportive. This story, though, begins after the race at the end of the post-race celebration dinner. My family and I were walking out of the tent when an overweight man came up to us. "What you did this weekend was so inspirational, and I came today to see you," he said.

Then he took out a full pack of cigarettes from his pocket and threw them into the trash can. He then told us all that he would never smoke again. I am sure my face registered the amazement I felt. He further said that I might see him on the same racecourse I'd ran sometime in the future.

I told him I was honored that he told me this and that I wished him the best of luck. Fast forward to 2015 when I was going for the Guinness World Record for most 70.3 *Half-Ironman* distance races in a year. One of the races was in Mont Tremblant. I was on the bike course when I heard someone call from behind me, "Fireman Rob, Fireman Rob. It's me."

The voice wasn't familiar, and I didn't want to turn around and crash into a wall. Suddenly, a man comes up beside me and says again, "Fireman Rob, it's me."

There he was, the man from 2013, just as he had promised. I had not spoken to him for two years.

"I lost one hundred and fifty pounds and I have not smoked since that day. I have been better for myself and for my family. I've totally changed my lifestyle. Thank you," he shouted, and he kept going.

He owned those promises he made two years before. Two thoughts surfaced at that moment; first, I was honored to have been a part of his journey, and second, there was no way I was going to catch him.

ACTION

The Fire represents you owning your excuses

The Logs are the excuse you need to OWN
EXCUSES for NOT OWNING Actions and words

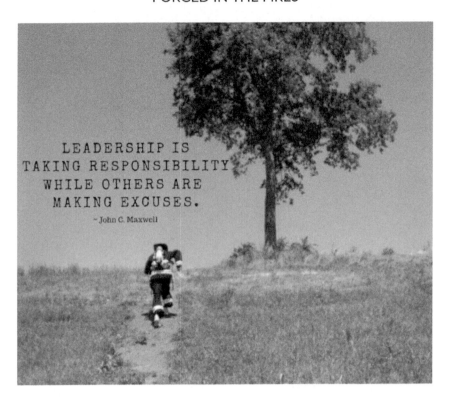

Chapter 5

3RD

CATALYST

DECISIONS

It's in your moments of decision that
your destiny is shaped.

Chapter 5:

DECISIONS – 3RD CATALYST

Making decisions with a strategy in mind is the only way to move forward purposefully and get the results we want. Our lives are a product of the decisions we make, whether consciously or subconsciously, on a daily basis. Sometimes, even deciding where to eat is a challenge, and making more significant decisions can be scary. Living up to the potential our lives have... well, that's what nightmares are made of. We can't abandon our dreams, but instead, pursue them with realistic decisions that move us forward. Our passionate purpose must be the compelling force that guides our decision-making.

At every fire scene, numerous dynamic situations occur simultaneously. Decisions need to be made in the NOW. Goals may change, as may circumstances, but decisions must be strategic. If the door is not available, I will use the window. My purpose is to save lives and all my decisions need to focus on that purpose. Ownership of my decisions and my resilience from previous successes and failures are a crucial part of the decisions I will make moving forward. I need to run into the fire, knowing that the bottom line is to **put the wet stuff on the red stuff,** or my crew and I are screwed.

Strategic decision-making is made from understanding our purpose and being willing to own our decisions. Critical, realistic thinking that prioritizes and focuses goals and consequent choices is empowering and gives us the chance to live to our true potential.

"Nothing happens by accident."

Making a decision can be a paralyzing event. Daily we make decisions about everything that affects our lives. Our lives are a result of our cumulative decisions and actions. We worry that the wrong decision will impact our future negatively, so we avoid making any decision at all. We need to understand that not everything will happen as we have designed it in our minds that we shouldn't abandon our dream or goal because we haven't made a decision that shows positive effects immediately. We need to decide to continue and move forward, knowing that our dreams and goals are worth pursuing.

The year was 2015 when I went for the Guinness World Record for the most 70.3 triathlons in a year. There were many logistics that came into that year. Flights, work, kids, all with me having to do 23 races that year. My decision to break the record created many problems that warranted additional decisions. It was harder than I ever thought it would be. Anyone who knows me knows that I am a scheduler and refer to it often. For me, making changes means that it has to flow with what is on the schedule, but we all know reality doesn't work that way. In 2015, I had four races that didn't work out for the world record.

The first race was one that was supposed to take place in Texas immediately after another race. I completed the race in a northern Texas that was brutally hot and totally kicked my butt. I then drove to Galveston for the second race. It was a long drive, and I didn't have much recovery time or sleep. So, when the morning came, I had to accept that I was unable to partake in the race in Galveston. That was one down on the schedule.

The second race was in Florida, and I found out, as I readied myself for the race, standing next to the sign that said, "No swimming due to gators," that the bike course had been shortened. The race wouldn't count for the record, so I didn't do it.

The third race was in Michigan. I had done the swim, had a great bike course, and was in transition. Boom! A vast thunder cloud rolled in and there I was in my gear ready to finish off this race with a 13.1-mile run. Then, Crack! Lightning! I pleaded with the director to let me go anyway. He assured me that with my tank, I was a clear target for the lightning, and the answer was "No."

At this point, my race decisions showed me three races down, but I had the race from Hell to come. It was a 24-hour race, meaning that I would leave my house and return home in less than 24 hours, after having done a race. I drove overnight to southern Illinois, arriving at about an hour before the start. It was a small race, but I needed to get enough races in my schedule to beat the record.

I was by myself for this race and the temperature was soaring near 99 degrees Fahrenheit. I decided not to wear the gear for the run portion of the race. I found out weeks later that they had shortened the bike course without telling me and I had done the race for nothing. I couldn't count it toward the record. However, I do believe that we make decisions and things happen for a reason. Maybe the decision I made not to wear my gear for that race and then it didn't count meant I was able to say that I did wear fire gear for all my world record races that counted. Maybe even better than that was that I then scheduled a race in Arizona.

I did a race to honor the 19 Granite Mountain hotshots who died battling a wildfire there. I was glad to be able to make the decision. The race was difficult due to the weight of the flag and the end of a long year of races, but with a mile left as I ran to the finish line to complete the race in time, I knew it was the right decision.

ACTION

<u>Who motivates you and Why?</u>

Photo of or Draw Your Support

Person _____

Why? _____

_____

_____

_____

Photo of or Draw Your Support

Person _____

Why? _____

_____

_____

_____

Photo of or Draw Your Support

Person _____

Why? _____

_____

_____

_____

"Set really small goals, enough to keep you going when every muscle in your body is screaming to quit."

The key to successful decision making is setting goals that are small and attainable. It is more functional to make small goals so that we feel we are moving along toward our bigger goals. Making decisions are not as scary when they are not so big. Small goals still need to be challenging, but if they are attainable, they will eventually make the overarching goal even more gratifying when reached. Smaller decisions make it easier to focus and succeed. If a decision doesn't work out, we can make a different one. We should not fear failure; we should fear indecision.

At the 2012 *Ironman Coeur d'Alene*, I met Ryan on the run portion of the triathlon. Every time I have raced there, I have met people who told me their incredible stories. While on the course along the lake, I started talking to Ryan. He was struggling, as was I. We had completed a 2.4-mile swim, a 112-mile bike and were nearing the end of a 26.2-mile marathon. Sometime after the race, someone forwarded a copy of a blog that Ryan had written to me.

> *I ran as long as I could run, and then I hit another wall. This wall was a little different because my brain wasn't working any longer. I kept trying to figure out my walk pace needed to be in order to finish in time. It was a SUFFERFEST for me and I wanted to know if I even had a chance. I couldn't even sum up 2+2 in my head. My brain wasn't working. I had told it to shut up about a thousand times during the day as it kept telling me to quit so it wasn't cooperating with me. I ran next to Fireman Rob, a famous Ironman who raises money for children's charities, and I introduced myself to him. I asked him if he could help me figure out what pace I needed to be in order to finish in time. He tried too, but his brain had also shut down. It was a somewhat comical moment where we both laughed about it and kept walking. He then said to me, Ryan... I'm going to tell you something, and you are going to have to trust me. You stay in front of me and you will finish in time.*

> *I quickly said, "How do you know that?"*

> *He then said with all the confidence in the world, "Because I have never not finished one of these."*

> *I believed! I heard what he said, I believed what he said, and now all I had to do was obey what he said.*

> *I used Fireman Rob as my pace car to make it to the cutoff. There would be times I would see him far ahead of me and I knew I needed to run so I would run and get back in front of*

him, knowing what he said to me meant I would finish. I believe with all my heart that God sent Fireman Rob to Coeur d'Alene just for me. Now, that may not be true, but it's what I believe. I learned to hear, believe, and obey, in that order. I also learned what hearing, believing and obeying can produce. At 16 hours, 20 minutes and 50 seconds (official time) I crossed that finish line in front of Fireman Rob.

As I crossed, I thanked Jesus for being with me that day and helping me through every single step. The name of this blog is **STAND FIRM TODAY.** *And although I could barely stand at all after that event, I learned something so incredibly valuable. God sends each of us people like Fireman Rob to help us Stand Firm.*

This story clearly delineates the essence of strategic decision making that Ryan had made in his countless decisions to run a little faster each time I caught up to him.

ACTION

<u>What are some of the daily small goals you will make a habit to move you towards the big goal?</u>

<u>Grocery List of Small Goals</u>

☐
☐
☐
☐
☐
☐
☐
☐
☐
☐

<u>Wish List for BIG GOAL</u>

I WILL...

1.

2.

3.

4.

5.

"Your strategic decision making will come from critical thinking forged in the fires of challenge and failure."

Becoming a strategic decision-maker comes from critical thinking when confronted with the fires of challenges and failures. The creation of a strategic mindset will come from our ability to create experiences, challenges and opportunities for ourselves. Being strategic doesn't necessarily mean well thought out, but rather well versed. It means having challenged life, not merely survived it. It means we may have made wrong decisions, suffered the consequences, caused others to suffer the consequences as well, but we have nonetheless learned to move forward. Our decision process must start and end with ourselves. It is within those moments when the fire gets bigger and hotter and we feel that hope has gone out the window, that we start to solidify how we will create our decisions moving forward. Every decision we make determines every other decision we make and thus we become strategic.

In St. George, Utah, at an *Ironman* race, the weather report was for 81 degrees with calm winds. Things seemed to be falling in place for a great race day. Then, midway through the swim, hurricane-force winds occurred in the reservoir, pushing five-foot swells, and making about 250 people to be taken out of the water. At times, I looked up to take a stroke, and water smashed me in the face; other times, I tried to take a stroke, there was no water, and I was thrown down three feet to the bottom of a swell. I was getting seasick, fighting the waves, and I vomited twice. So much for 81 degrees and calm winds.

After making it through the swim, I went onto the bike part of the race. Thirty miles in, the devil winds began, and that, coupled with the altitude, 6000 feet, conspired against my breathing. I struggled to stay on the road and breathe simultaneously. There was a hill called "The Wall" which taunted cyclists with its severe vertical ascent that came directly after a hairpin curve so that no one could build up any speed at all. My inner voice was talking to me, trying hard to convince myself that I needed to keep going. On the last downhill to the finish line, I decided that I had to go as fast as possible to make the finish time for the bike. I was passing cars and my bike was shaking. Possibly a shaky decision?

I did survive and began the run in my fifty pounds of gear. My body was so exhausted at that point, and I had a marathon staring me in the face, with hills, heat and wind. I decided to run a bit, something difficult to do in gear, and walking 15-minute miles for over 19 miles. It became obvious that I was not going to finish by midnight.

It was then that I made another decision; I was going to finish the marathon, however long it took. The decision to never give up led me to the finish line at 1:00 a.m., exhausted and exhilarated. I knew that my children would be proud, and when I spoke with them about it later, they would learn the importance of doing their best and never giving up. The decision to finish the race was momentous for me and helped me learn that I could push myself to achieve things beyond what seemed logical. It taught me that my decisions would lead me to the great conclusion that never giving up is always worth more than finishing on time. A strategic way forward!

ACTION

Habits you have or want to make critical decisions.

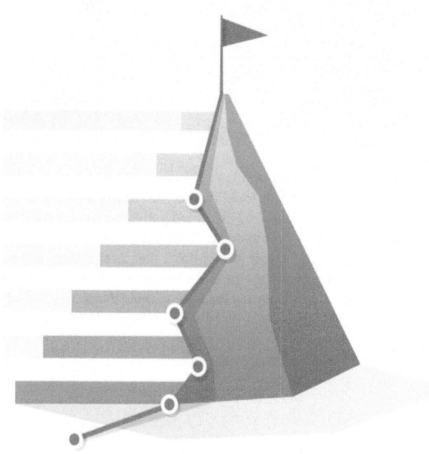

Write your habits in the lines, that help you climb the decision mountain

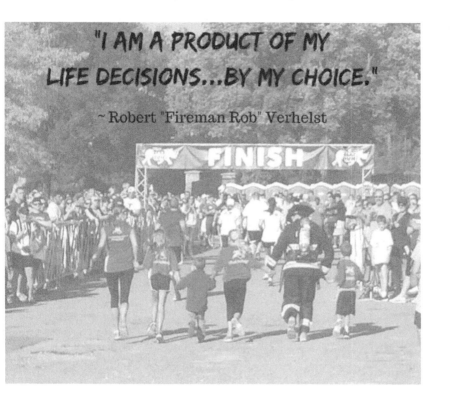

"I AM A PRODUCT OF MY
LIFE DECISIONS....BY MY CHOICE."

~ Robert "Fireman Rob" Verhelst

Chapter 6

EMOTIONAL CONTROL

If you want to do something, you find a way. If you don't want to do something you find an excuse.

Chapter 6:

EMOTIONAL CONTROL – 4TH CATALYST

Sometimes people will refer to an out of control situation as akin to herding cats, occasionally frightening, and sometimes comical. Out of control emotions, however, are destructive and dangerous. We must confront adverse events with emotional control, taking power from them and using it to develop resiliency and understanding. Emotions are valid and controlling our reaction to those emotions makes them productive in creating who we are as people. Not allowing the negatives that come into our lives, neither to define us nor to destroy us, builds our emotional control.

The fire service tests one's emotional control profoundly. Managing our emotions is imperative, both at the scene and after. Bad moments, stressors, or fears can't be piled up and stored somewhere to ignore them. They all need to be acknowledged and managed. Emotions are powerful and try to subvert control but turning control back on our emotions gives us power and command of the situation. In a fire, we need to maintain our **offensive attack**, fighting the fire head-on and not letting it dictate our path. We make the rules and don't let up. If we are defensive without cause, we let the fire dictate our movements, our path in our lives.

Are we ever going to be in total control of our emotions? NO WAY! They are an essential part of what makes us human. In pursuit of our goals, there are times when challenges will assault our emotions, forcing us to reframe our minds, believe in ourselves and persistently confront the excuses and desire to bail out. It is at this moment that we call on our resilience, self-confidence and strength from our passion for taking control and making emotionally controlled decisions and actions.

"Negative thoughts are inevitable, yet the reaction to them is manageable."

Negative thoughts are inevitable, yet we need our reaction to them to be manageable. Throughout our lives, we will encounter many negative thoughts that seek to derail our goals and dreams. We must develop an effective manner in which to handle these thoughts. This is not easy, nor will we ever be perfect at handling them. It is not that we are not in control of our thoughts, but instead, we **can** control them. Just as in decision making, we must shape our emotional reactions.

I remember the day I returned from 9/11, getting home and feeling like I was floating, and I couldn't focus on anything that was going on. My life fell apart, gradually creating change that didn't help me one bit dealing with the crap that was overtaking every part of me. I would go into the firehouse and I would hear from others, "You seem different," or "Wow, you are not the same person, Rob."

These comments were so not helpful at the time. I couldn't even help myself and yet it seemed like others were helping to push me more towards the cliff I so wanted to jump off.

"What do I do? What can I do? Who the Hell am I? Is it worth it?" All of these things have run through my head countless times throughout my life. That feeling of hopelessness is only one part of what makes PTSD seem like cancer that invades our bodies.

The way I see PTSD for me is that it is like having closets full of photos, videos, and other materials from my life. Now, these are not like the nicely labeled family home movies that fit easily on a shelf and brought out for viewing when one wants to smile and laugh. These items in my closet don't stack neatly, don't fit nicely in the closet and every once in a while, fall out and hit me in the head when I am trying to close the door. That's not even the worst part. I don't only have one closet. I have multiple closets and they continue to add up every time I work at the firehouse.

So, now, I have a problem, yet this problem is considered in my profession and in other occupations like mine, military and police, to be more a badge of shame. "I don't want this label. What will people think of me? They'll think I am crazy and need help?"

Well, they were right.

ACTION

<u>Emotional Control can be like a ladder with some broken rungs</u>

Focus on using the positives to get past the negatives.

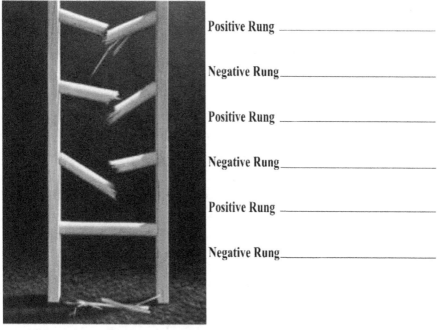

Positive Rung _____

Negative Rung_____

Positive Rung _____

Negative Rung_____

Positive Rung _____

Negative Rung_____

Write either a Trait, Situation, or Emotion that you see as a positive rung to move

forward and a negative rung that you need to get past.

"You never change things by fighting
the existing reality."

~BUCKMINSTER FULLER

When trying to achieve emotional control, there is often an external source that is meddling with our equilibrium. This source may be pushing us "over the edge" toward a loss of control. It is interesting to note that an existing reality is often the culprit that interferes with our emotions. We can't keep running into the same wall, thinking that we will run through it. We can't keep taking the same path if it doesn't lead where we want to go. We need to look at an awkward situation, not as a hurdle or problem, but as a means to grow and learn. We can't continue to fight the existing reality that we may or may not be able to control; we need to control our emotional responses to what we do or feel and find a way to move forward.

I made a trip down to San Antonio to go with Southwest Airlines employees to deliver teddy bears from the Fireman Rob Foundation to kids at the Methodist Children's Hospital of South Texas. It is always an amazing experience when I get to deliver the bears with our Ambassadors. On this occasion, I brought along a medal from one of my races. This medal was crazy big. It looked like something Mr. T would wear. I was saving this for a little kid who truly needed it. I didn't have any idea as to who that would be or what they needed to be like. It was just an option. We got to the first room and all of us went in.

"Hi. I'm Fireman Rob from the Fireman Rob Foundation. We are here to give your daughter this bear. Would that be okay?"

The mom came up to us, holding back the tears, and said, "She could use that right now."

We walked up to the bed. "Hi. I'm Rob. I wanted to give you a bear, and I hope you feel better soon."

She grabbed the bear, hugged it in close, and rolled over, facing away from us. I thanked the mom and walked out.

"How do you do this?" asked one of the Southwest employees.

"What do you mean?"

"I... I...

I felt extremely bad for the little girl and her mom and the girl started to tear up. I had to say something. "It's important. What you're feeling is even more important. It's about giving each family, each child a smile. I wish I could make them better and I hope that this is a small part of that."

She nodded her head, and we continued delivering bear after bear. Finally, we got to a room of a little girl about six years old who was by herself. The nurse told us a little about the girl's situation. "She's been here for a month. Her parents have to work all day, so she is usually here for long periods of time alone."

This was the one. The nurse didn't want all of us to go in there. The Southwest people looked at me, "Rob, you go in."

I walked in, thinking about my kids being in that room alone.

"Hi. I'm Fireman Rob. I have two things to give you."

The nurse had told me that she was not especially talkative. She looked at me with a guarded smile.

"First, I want to give you this bear." Her eyes lit up, and her arms went straight out to hug the bear.

"But that isn't all. I have a special medal for you."

She started to smile again, and then it was a smile like Christmas morning.

"This is a medal for courage, for you. I have been told, you are *soooo* strong."

She giggled a little, still not saying a word.

"Do you want to wear it?"

She nodded vigorously. I put the medal over her head, and it covered most of her body. "It was so amazing to meet you. You keep strong, okay."

Then she stood up and with the same arms wide open as she had done when I gave her the bear, softly voiced, "Thank you."

I hugged her and instantly knew why we deliver bears. I wasn't going to cure her problem; I wasn't even going to be the long-term solution. But, at that moment, it was the best cure possible... a SMILE.

ACTION

<u>What existing reality are you trying to fight?</u>

How can you change your perspective to move through it?

1. _____

Change _____

_____

2. _____

Change _____

_____

3. _____

Change _____

_____

Write down the existing reality (situation or thought) that is holding you back,

then write the change or changes in perspective you will make to move forward

"The secret is what psychologists call habituation. Meaning the more you're exposed to something that you initially fear, then the less you will fear it and eventually, you become immune to it. You get used to it."

The secret is what psychologists call "habituation." The more we are exposed to something that we initially fear, we eventually become used to it, and immune to it. Sometimes, to succeed, we need to stay in situations that are painful or challenging, always bearing in mind our purpose, while not allowing ourselves to be unduly harmed in an unsafe situation that hurts more than helps. Habituation takes time to develop since it is our willingness to stay in a situation without losing control of ourselves or our direction. Physical endurance and the control of emotional negativity are two components for creating habituation. Controlling our emotional negatives will help us find that clear path that may be covered up; it will help us understand if we need to exit the situation if it is not leading us in the right direction. Habituation can be the tool that allows us to move toward our goal, to realize that the discomfort of challenge can lead to success.

In the fire service or in my triathlon life, habituation is a crucial component in my ability to achieve my goal. Emotional control can mean the difference between life and death, something I realized as a twenty-two-year-old on my first call, where there was a PNB (Pulseless non-breather). I had been trained well and as I performed CPR on the person, I looked into the person's eyes. There was no life. Where had the person gone? It was the first experience of life leaving right before my eyes. I remember not being able to understand or even rationalize it in my mind. I still can't; yet, with each shift and each trauma, I learned the importance of doing my job with my emotions in check.

One morning in 2012, at the *Ironman World Championship* in Kona, Hawaii, my wife, Nicole, and I were honored to have breakfast with Scott, the first double amputee to finish the *Ironman World Championship*. Sitting at a beautiful restaurant overlooking the ocean and pier area where the race would begin on Sunday morning, we noticed a helicopter flying north to sound really low near the water.

"What is that helicopter doing? It's crazy low."

Scott answers me, "Well, they do that with the helicopter to scare the sharks away. The vibrations from the helicopters on the water supposedly scare them away."

"There are sharks in the bay area here?" I query, recalling my fear when I was told not to stray from the other swimmers in San Francisco Bay during Escape from Alcatraz for fear of the sharks, or when I swam across Tampa Bay in honor of Navy Seals and a kayaker stayed with me to scare off sharks with his paddle. I breathe deeply, thinking about the sharks.

Then Scott says, "I wouldn't worry too much about it. There are about four amputees in the race, so the sharks will think they were already here."

Humor can be wonderful. Little moments of levity can bring a balance to our emotions.

ACTION

**Write you fears you have under the water
and the good habits next to the life preserver that keeps you afloat.**

GOOD HABITS

FEARS

Two things define you. Your patience when you have nothing, and your attitude when you have everything.

Chapter 7

5<small>TH</small>
CATALYST

RESILIENCE

Show up and keep showing up. One day
you'll look up and you'll be in front of
the line.

Chapter 7:

RESILIENCE – 5TH CATALYST

Resilience is built, not by pleasant occurrences, but rather by discomforting and painful events. It's easy to bail out and avoid moving forward when it becomes difficult to do so. A resilient person tolerates the discomfort for a greater purpose and wills himself/herself through less than ideal situations. This does not mean staying in conditions that cause undue pain or danger, or that are misaligned with one's passion or purpose. Resilient people have faith in themselves that they can endure because they are capable and strong enough to overcome challenging situations.

At a fire scene, why would we **run into the fire**? With temperatures in most house fires burning as hot as 1100 degrees on the ceiling and 600 degrees where we are standing, the desire to bailout would be strong. Yet, a resiliency is built up through our training in this austere environment, coupled with a firm belief in our purpose, which gives us the desire to persevere. Most people couldn't imagine even choosing to stay close to the conditions of a fire, yet the resiliency that is built in a firefighter from his experience and difficulty while on the job overcomes all.

Using the difficulties, the pain, the disappointments and mistakes to grow stronger and more resilient is necessary for moving forward toward our purpose. Following our passion demands a resilient and positive outlook minus fear because we have learned through experience that we can prevail over adversity. We are empowered through believing in ourselves and by our commitment to our purpose. We are ready to **run into the fire.**

"You have the ability to rationalize anything
in your head."

Resilience is endurance and the ability to rationalize to endure. Our ability to frame our reality to allow ourselves to push forward is the basis of resiliency. It is the accumulation of behaviors that don't let us give up, that makes us learn and grow from taking ownership in our decision; decisions that no one else makes for fear of failure or pain. Resiliency is a powerful force within us that permits us to rationalize the impossible in our minds, to find the positives amidst the negatives.

There are many stories of the events that have contributed to my personal development of resiliency.

The first one occurred in the days after 9/11 when I worked in search and recovery on the pile of the World Trade Center.

"I need to step off for a minute."

The area chief waved his hand, and I walked off the pile through the guarded entry onto Church Street. Each step I took was simply muscle memory. No destination. No sightseeing. I was just walking.

I heard from behind me, "Sir! Sir!"

I felt a hand on my shoulder. The smell of a freshly roasted chicken hit my nostrils. A lady holding a whole, cooked chicken in a plastic container was standing there, holding out a chicken to me. "Sir, I bought four of these." She shoved a chicken toward me. "I don't cook. I gave the three others to other workers and I want you to have this one."

I paused for a second, trying to wrap my head around this amazing gesture.

"Wow. Um. Thank you so much. I greatly appreciate this." I sat down on a curb, opened up the container, and instantly, I was far away from Ground Zero. My mind moved me to Thanksgiving with my family, and a wave of positive emotion surged through me. I looked up one more time to see the lady's smiling face as she walked away.

I shouted after her, "Thank you." This incident is only one of many 9/11 memories that still haunt my thoughts, but I can always smile about the kindness that came out of the horror.

Throughout my life, in the darkest of times, there have been small events like this that have smothered the raging fire of pain and defeat and allowed me to endure the reality of the moment by framing it in positivity. There was a race in Florida in 2015, during the time of the year with unbearable heat. Not exactly a surprise. On the run, while I walked in gear as vigorously as I could manage, the water stations were seemingly miles and miles apart. It was not easy to endure between them, but then, there they were, coming toward me, five girls, a cup with water in each hand. They knew my struggle and didn't want me to wait until I reached the water station. They came out on the course to meet me. Just as a firefighter hoses down a fire, these kind people brought water to a firefighter, showed him hope, and built his resilience.

ACTION

What is a moment in your life you learned through being resilient? Why did you do it?

MOMENT

WHY?

MOMENT

WHY?

MOMENT

WHY?

"Mountaintops inspire leaders, but
valleys mature them."

~WINSTON CHURCHILL

It is often said that life is a series of peaks and valleys. Success, achievement, and awards are all at the mountaintop. It is great when we are up there, and we feel like we can do anything. If that is taken away, or we start to slip, do we panic?

Life does not always consist of mountaintops, and sometimes they're even few and far between. For the most part, we all live in the valleys, working our way up to one of those mountaintops. Our valleys need to be places of growth, not of fear, sadness, or despair. We are continually working to better ourselves and define our new potential. We should enjoy the mountaintops that we dream of when we achieve them, not be disheartened when we don't quite get there, but continue to be resilient and grow. Either we are growing, or we are dying.

This was to be my mountaintop. As 2016 rolled around, I noted that *Ironman Wisconsin* would be on September 11th, the 15th anniversary of 9/11. After having achieved the Guinness World Record in 2015, my body was depleted, but the disconnect between what my body was telling me and what my heart and mind wanted to do was an absolute chasm. It seemed that this race in Madison, where I had begun to race as Fireman Rob, would complete my journey.

My preparation for this "last" race was less than impressive, yet, I was sure I could do it. There were, however, many factors that came into the picture late in my race preparation. I had a commitment that brought me back into Madison by 9:50 p.m. on Saturday, with the race to begin the next morning. I quickly packed my gear. My mind kept asking, "Am I ready for this?"

This was the most scared I ever felt before a race. I was putting pressure on myself to make this something special.

Nicole asked, "How are you feeling this morning, honey?"

"Like it's the first race of my life..."

"What?"

"I've never been as nervous as I am right now."

There was a film crew doing a documentary of the day and that meant the day started at 4:00 a.m. -- nothing like adding to the pressure. The film crew asked me questions, such as, "What does this day mean to you?"

Every time I tried to respond, the tears welled in my eyes and I couldn't speak. I began, "I am so honored..."

This was the start of my day, not boding well for the long day to come.

We arrived at the race, and I was poignantly aware of the fact that I had not even been there to put my gear into the transition area since I had been out of town since Wednesday of that week. This was nerve-racking for me since it was so foreign to my pre-race behavior. I repeatedly heard, "Good luck, Fireman Rob," coming through the dark of the early morning, adding to my emotions.

I was asked, "What does this day mean to you?"

I was unable to answer without crying. I began to worry about a salt deficiency due to all the crying.

I reached the race start, a 2.4-mile swim in beautiful Lake Monona. Beautiful here is defined as full of algae and seaweed, where you can barely see your hand in front of your face. Mike Reilly, the voice of *Ironman,* said, "The only thing you can control today is your attitude."

Then, "BANG!" the cannon shattered the still morning and a mass start of 3,000 hopeful friends I swam with, and past over one another, making the event resemble a *WrestleMania* gone wild. Having played water polo in college, I enjoyed the experience. Staying in my head, and not allowing all the splash and distance of the swim to disrupt my race meant that I needed to turn on what I called, "Rob TV." It was my personal television program made up of planning my life and reflecting on recent events. No one else would ever want to watch this program; I am sure, but it got me through the hour and 20 minutes it usually takes me to complete the swim.

I exited the water and felt great thinking that this could be one of my best races. Running to the bike, I told myself, "All you have to do is finish the one hundred and twelve miles on the bike, and then run, you'll be motivated by everybody to be able to finish."

I took my time in transition to get on my bike shorts, and I headed out on the bike. At about fifteen miles into the bike portion of the race, I knew something was wrong. My energy was drained. I felt as if I had biked into an abyss. My motivation had slipped, and for some reason, the dark moments that usually didn't come until later in the race started to become more prevalent in my mind. I kept my mind from going to the questions, "What is going on? What am I doing here?" I stopped at every aid station sitting in the porta-potties, trying to convince myself to keep racing. This race was supposed to be the mountaintop, but it was becoming a deep dark valley. How could this be happening? I kept going as I pushed through it determined to finish.

I reached one of the big hills on the course about at the 40-mile mark. This hill had a 14% grade. On the right side of the road, it looked like ants marching their bikes up the side, fifty strong. One other individual and I were biking, almost going backward, but biking nonetheless up the hill. My lungs burned, my legs tightened like rubber bands, and then, out of nowhere, chest pain overtook me. I kept going, anyway. This was the beginning of the end and I not only knew it, I also felt it.

I went about another ten miles and the camera crew caught up with me on their motorcycle. "How you are feeling, Rob?"

"Awful."

"What's going on?"

"Chest is tight, my legs are tight, my back is tight. I am just in pain."

"Is it emotional, or are you in too much pain?"

"To be honest, I'm in too much pain."

They filmed for a few more miles, and then I was back in my head again trying to convince my body to continue. I saw my family which brought reality to my thoughts. *You don't have an option. You are leading by example. DO NOT STOP.* ran through my mind while my body yelled at me. I couldn't breathe; by back was in so much pain; I had cramps in both legs, and I was starting to see a black ring on the outside of my vision. This was not normal.

But... as every crazy dreamer who wants to create change would do... I continued out on the second loop. This would prove to be my demise. My thoughts evaded me completely. It felt like I was riding very slowly through a tunnel. My pedals were barely moving, my mind unable to focus on anything other than the road in front of my tire. I don't remember much until the wheels fell off... not the ones on the bike, but those running throughout my body. My chest pain returned along with my asthma that I battled throughout the day.

"Just keep pedaling," was all I could say to myself. Then, as I ascended a slight uphill... my motor stopped... my brain's message to my legs did not get through, and I started traveling backward. I could no longer reason nor physically control what was about to happen. I was drifting backward, and I turned the wheel, crossing the road; not smart. I headed through a ditch and onto a patch of grass, where I collapsed to the ground and lay.

Here I was, an 18-time *Ironman* finisher, Guinness World Record Holder for most half-distance races, and I was DONE... DONE!

My purpose to inspire on the anniversary of 9/11 ...DONE!

My kids seeing their dad complete what he had started ...DONE!

At that moment, I couldn't even think about it. I was having chest pain, and I was scared like I had never been before.

For the next 24 hours, I was at the hospital, where they tested my heart and other functions. Along with that stress, I was sitting there, knowing that my career as Fireman Rob running *Ironman* triathlons in full fire gear for the run portions was over, but not in the way I would have liked it to end. I didn't even get to the run portion.

Perspective is like a swift kick in the ass. While I was sitting there, I also realized that I gave everything I had, and my family said they loved me.

I learned the greatest lesson of all -- failure can be a success if we don't let our stupidity cloud our perspective.

I ended up getting discharged from the hospital the next day. My heart was clear. The doctor came in, and said, "Besides the obvious of being a little crazy, what happened is that you have a torn intercostal muscle that mimicked heart chest pain. Then, with your asthma acting up through the day and you using your inhaler, your heart rate was way beyond your normal limits. All this led to your legs not working; in other words, exercise-induced collapse. This happens a lot in dogs when they run in circles over and over."

I didn't find the mountaintop, but my valley was not as low as I worried it might be, and I grew in resilience.

I was thinking to myself; *I have been diagnosed with a human malady, but I have been compared to my dog.*

Perspective.

ACTION

Write the Leadership trait you want at the mountaintop
Write the challenge(s) you foresee or have to reach them.

LEADERSHIP _____

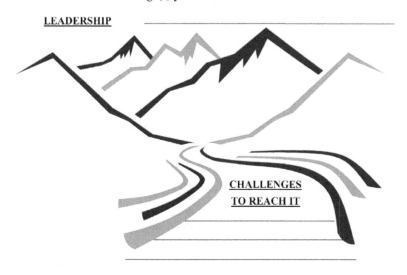

**CHALLENGES
TO REACH IT**

LEADERSHIP _____

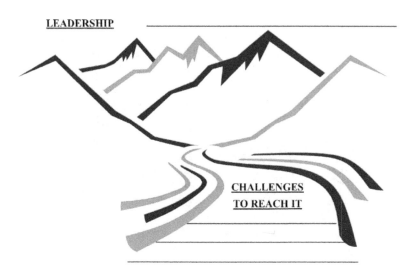

**CHALLENGES
TO REACH IT**

"One of the biggest ways you can build resilience to the things that come your way is to manage your expectations."

One of the biggest to build resilience is to do things that come your way is to manage your expectations. Too often, when we go for big goals, we look at the mountaintop and fail to see all the hills, valleys and plateaus along the way. We need to replace our expectations based on the end result and build our resilience based on smaller goals and a shorter path. Expectations are a scary thing since they are not always based on our experiences, but rather on other people's experiences who may or may not have the same abilities that we do. Personal resilience depends on expectations according to our own path, our journey and our dedication. Since resiliency is built on experiences that push us out of our comfort zone, expectations play a huge role in not just helping us to focus, but also in allowing us to grow.

In 2015 I participated in the *Miami Man Triathlon* at the Homestead Miami Racetrack. This day tested my mental strength to the ultimate. It was an oppressively hot Florida day. This was the 10th race of the

2015 season, where I would set the Guinness World Record. The swim was uneventful, and I exited in my usual time. I went out on the bike course, poignantly aware of the debilitating heat that was pressing down on me. I then discovered that the temperature was not the worst thing I would be fighting that day. My bike seat was broken and would not stay in place. I spent the next 56 miles standing on my bike, unable to sit on the seat because it would drop to its lowest point every time I sat on it.

By the time I transitioned to the run, I was feeling sick. My mind kept asking me what I was doing. I had to respond, "One step at a time." As I walked in all my gear in the blistering heat, my stomach did somersaults. I needed to stop and vomit, but that didn't help. At one point, I stopped. My mom was tracking me, and she was there. I took off my tank and sat against a fence. This was the point at which all the work I had done to get to this part of the race throughout the year came crashing down and my mind was yelling at me, "This pain is too much. Stop the insanity."

Then another part of my resilient mind yelled back, "You can finish what you started. Just keep going."

My mom didn't say much since she was only there to support whatever I decided to do. I'm sure her mind was yelling for me to stop. She knew it was my decision, and I had to take ownership of the situation and decide for myself. I picked up the tank, paused, and set it back down.

Today, I needed to finish without the tank, the first time, ever. I started again, one step at a time. I think I vomited about five times on that race. When I had one mile left into the entrance of the racetrack, two police officers parked their cars and told me they would walk with me to the finish line. Mental strength is also about allowing others to be there for you and to use their strength to help you with yours. We walked to the finish line.

A part of me was surprised that I had done this, but I was proud I had persevered. We may fall on our faces a few times to learn the limits of our mental strength, to learn how to adapt the limits, and how to persevere through perceived limits. Our mind, our thoughts are our most powerful force to advance or retreat.

ACTION

Write the top four expectations of yourself.

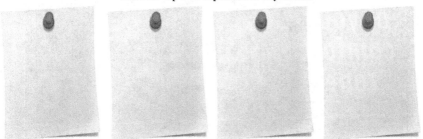

Write if the above expectations are REAL or FAKE and Why.

Chapter 8

FAITH OVER FEAR

A belief is nothing more than a feeling of absolute certainty about what something means. Beliefs control our behavior.

Chapter 8:

FAITH OVER FEAR – 6TH CATALYST

Why are some people fearful of trying something new, while some people are searching for opportunities to do the impossible? It's all about faith over fear, believing in ourselves, our abilities, and our path, not allowing fear of failure to subdue faith in ourselves. Empowering fear removes our power, creating a culture of excuses and stagnation. There will inevitably be mistakes but fearing them strengthens them and diminishes our own strength. We must focus on our ability to do the work, trust that we will do our best and gain positively from what we do.

In the fire service, we must maintain a high level of faith in ourselves and our brothers and sisters, since going home at the end of shift depends on it. When someone is trapped in a mangled car, and they look at me for help, that person's faith in me and my faith in myself are essential for a successful **extrication**. This seems like an extreme example, but is it really? Isn't faith in oneself and each other what gives us the strength and courage to **run into the fire** literally and figuratively? We are called firefighters, not because we don't fear fire, but because we fight it with a purpose-driven faith that it won't get the best of us.

All the strategic decisions made in life or at a fire scene are made believing that they are the best decision for that situation. If there is an error in judgment, it can be disastrous for a firefighter, but a decision must be made, nonetheless, using faith over fear and trusting that as a team, my brothers, sisters and I will ultimately win. So too, mistakes that are made and actions that don't warrant desired results are part of life, but believing in ourselves, we make them useful tools to grow. **Bailing out** because of fear is not an option. Using a **fireproof** faith in ourselves to live to our truest potential will burn fear to the ground.

"When I talk about faith, it is the essence of confidence and belief in yourself, your abilities and your path."

I think of faith as the essence of confidence and belief in myself, my abilities, and my chosen path. Two critical components of success are faith in myself and the belief that I am capable of overcoming any fears or obstacles. My faith is built on trust having been in those situations where I am the only one who will move me forward. It is in that moment that I create the trust in myself to make the right decisions. Faith is belief beyond the fear that things will turn out okay, whether now or later. Fear can deter my progress, or if tempered by faith, motivate me. I determine which path I take, one of faith or one of fear.

"Get up and get out! Let's go. Let's go. Let's go. Daylight is burning."

My time in the military was one of the most rewarding times in my life. I learned what being part of something bigger than myself meant. I understand why we have the freedoms we do and what the cost is. When I enlisted, I was lost, not looking for direction, but rather for purpose. Post 9/11. Post-divorce.

I was twenty-four years old and going through Air Force basic training at Lackland Air Force Base in (always hot) San Antonio, Texas. My life was flipped upside down, and each day was scripted. Basically, my freedom to make choices gone. I was fighting for the freedom we all enjoy, my country controlling my life.

Being older than most of the recruits, I was looked upon as the person who needed to help the younger recruits adjust to life in the military. My own needs were sublimated to their needs. Many of them were leaving poverty, abusive situations, hopeless futures, and failing lives.

Near the end of basic training, during our downtime in the evening, a young airman, with his head in his hands, was sitting by his footlocker.

"What's going on, Michael?" I asked.

He was getting choked up, trying not to show his emotion, so I sat down next to him. He still couldn't talk.

"Michael, it's okay, brother. Talk to me. What is going on?"

We were two weeks from graduating basic training, and by this time, our minds were focused on our mission ...becoming Airmen. We needed to get it together. I felt the responsibility to help my fellow recruits fulfill this mission. I pushed my demons aside and made my priority getting our flight through.

"I...I...I can't do this. I am worthless."

"Bullshit," I said. "Michael, you are worth it."

"No, you don't understand. My dad was a fireman, and I didn't know what to do after high school, so this is where I went. Now I don't know if I can."

"If you can do what? We are almost done. I know you can. Here ...one second..."

His dad was a fireman in New York. He lived in New York during 9/11, and his dad volunteered during those days. Michael felt worthless and fearful, unaware of his purpose. I went into my footlocker to get out my purpose. In a little yellow bag, I had a small cloth flag that I had worn on my helmet during my time at 9/11. Sewn on the corner was a part of the baby blanket I had found on my last day on the pile. Over the last months, I had used this when the demons were knocking down the door. I used it to give me a perspective not to give up. This meant everything to me, but at this moment, Michael needed it.

We need to give each other the faith to overcome our fears.

"I know you don't see who you are, but I believe in you, and well, I want to give you something, but you need to promise me something. You need to promise me that you will not question yourself. I know you."

Opening the yellow bag, I felt a strange emotion sweep through my body. I was parting with a huge piece of me, embodied in a small United States flag. I handed him the flag. He knew my story. "This is my purpose. Now it's yours. Finish this and finish strong. If not for you, for me."

He took it, looked me in the eye, and nodded.

Michael finished basic training, went on to be an Air Force firefighter, and then have a career in New York. To be honest, I miss that flag and everything it gave me and stood for. I wish I could have kept it, but it was not meant for me to keep. I needed to move forward on my own without it. I know the impact of 9/11 on me will never go away, but I also know just as Michael is worth it, so am I worth every minute I live. My impact is not in the big things I have accomplished, but rather the little things I do that I never planned to do, living faith over fear every day.

ACTION

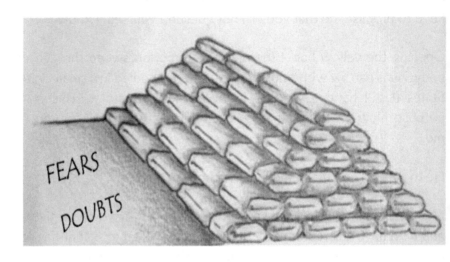

The Sandbags are your strengths
that hold back your fears & doubts.

"The more we empower fear and enable dismissal (sweep it under the rug), the less we empower ourselves to overcome now and in the future."

The more we empower fear and enable dismissal, sweeping it under the rug, the less we empower ourselves to overcome now and in the future. For the most part, our comfort zones are where we stay since it is easier to give in or give up than it is to stick it out. We can't let our fears control our lives, just as our excuses shouldn't dictate our path. We have been taught the value of a linear path through life, one that minimizes pain, but do we truly reach our growth potential on this path? Throughout my life, I have challenged myself, not allowing fear to determine the results, not letting myself make excuses for the results. The crucial component of faith over fear is to consistently strive to keep fear from prescribing the path and let faith move us toward our goals.

Imagine being lost in your own life. No feeling of direction or belonging. Feeling like you missed the last boat leaving to take you to the rest of your life. This was me to a T. My mind was full of trauma and negatives that were building someone I didn't know. I sucked. Then, it happened. That impact moment that changed my life forever.

I'll take you back to 2011. It is Sept 11th and the 10th anniversary of the 9/11 attacks. Why is this of importance? I was there doing search and recovery two days after the attacks. The days felt like a lifetime at the age of twenty-three. For years, I dealt with the demons that would override life until Sept 11th in 2011.

I didn't realize it at the moment when I decided to race *Ironman Wisconsin* to commemorate those who lost their lives on that day and to inspire others to follow their passions. For those of you who don't know, an *Ironman* is a 2.4-mile swim, 112-mile bike and to truly impact those watching; I wore fifty pounds of firefighter gear for the 26.2-mile run ...more of a walk for me. The gear included the helmet, turnout coat, bunker pants and SCBA or breathing apparatus.

This day proved to be a turning point in my life. It taught me the meaning of life -- my life and that my life was a product of my mind. The first race I ever did in gear was to test if I could actually do it. I remember this sweltering hot day like it was yesterday. Racine, Wisconsin. The host of an *Ironman* 70.3 ...half the distance of the full race, I was doing in September. Now to give you the Cliff notes of a triathlon -- the swim is wet, and the bike is windy and long as Hell. Most of my stories begin when I went into the changing tent as Clark Kent or Robert Verhelst and came out Superman or "Fireman Rob."

This day challenged my sanity, with it being a 110-degree index day. I was putting on an all-black gear that weighed as much as a backpack full of five medium-sized bowling balls. Looking back, I can't help but wonder what the hell I was thinking.

Either way, I went to my bag in transition and got out the black firefighter gear and put it on, slowly feeling the weight added to my shoulders and the oppressive heat as each piece of clothing suffocated the airflow to my body. Through the pain, I continued, yet my mind was doubting my ability and purpose until ...I was about four miles into the course and another athlete running on the other side crossed over stopping me in my tracks with a hug. As he hugged me with a feeling of needing support, he said, "I'm a retired FDNY firefighter, because of 9/11. Thank you so much for remembering our brothers. What you are doing is so important."

It was that comment I needed to change my mindset from a poor me to a get it done attitude. This transferred not only to the future races I did, but also to me in my personal life.

ACTION

List your fears, egos, excuses and why, then check the box if you want to change it.

Fear

☐ _____

☐ _____

☐ _____

Ego

☐ _____

☐ _____

☐ _____

Excuse

☐ _____

☐ _____

☐ _____

"You must be willing to focus on your ability to do the work without fear of falling or failure."

One of the most important attributes we can possess is our willingness to work. It is not only crucial to work, not just physically, but also mentally. If the work appears to be a failure, this is not as important as whether or not we haven't given up. Sometimes the fear of failure stops us from working, but we need to trust ourselves that, in the end, we will be okay. The faith in our work starts in our minds and moves through our bodies to move us forward. Believing in ourselves gives us the strength to do the work to lead us to success.

At *Ironman Wisconsin* 2011. It was the 10th anniversary of 9/11, and I was doing my first *Ironman* with full firefighter gear for the 26.2 miles run of this race. Yet, before I could get to this part, I had to finish the 2.4-mile swim and 112-mile bike.

101

I got out of the swim, "Great work! Transition this way!"

I switched into my bike gear and ran toward my bike.

I felt good. I knew what lay in front of me on the 112-mile ride …I was about fifteen miles into the 112-mile bike, and I was hungry.

"What the…Where's my food? Are you kidding me?"

All my nutrition had fallen out of my gear in transition. I had nothing.

Keep in mind that the reason most athletes don't finish *Ironman* is BAD nutrition. Great start to a long day ahead of me. The catering on the bike course had bananas and this stuff that tasted like …well …I couldn't feed it to my dog.

There I was …no food …over ninety miles to ride, then a marathon in 50 pounds of gear.

Then, at mile 85, I saw it …a bagel …visible from the back pocket of another rider's jersey. She was just ahead of me …only about 10 yards but in the middle of the hill …I had just started to climb.

Thoughts ran through my head. *Knock her down and take the bagel …No, No, No … I'll just catch her and ask for it.*

"CATCH HER???" my ailing body chimed in.

"We are barely just surviving, and you want me to do what?"

Mind over matter …I decided to charge up the hill with every last ounce of energy left. It felt like it took an hour to catch her.

Out of breath, I asked, "Can I have your bagel?"

She said, "Totally! It has to be stale, but you can definitely have it."

"Thanks." I grabbed the bagel from her hand as if it were a precious jewel and slowed down to a snail's pace.

It had the consistency of a table, but it tasted like survival.

ACTION

The following characteristic shovels can dig you out of
your doubts, egos and fears.

List the qualities within these characteristics that you want to develop

WORK	TRUST	RESILIENCE
_____	_____	_____
_____	_____	_____
_____	_____	_____
_____	_____	_____

"TRUST YOURSELF
when no one else does."

Chapter 9

7TH CATALYST

MENTAL STRENGTH

Mental Strength is survival...
it is opportunity...it is happiness and it is
who we are and can be.

Chapter 9:

MENTAL STRENGTH – 7TH CATALYST

Are we tough? What can we endure? Mentally tough people trust themselves. They know that there are limits, but they are pushing those perceived limits, persevering in the face of what others might deem impossible. Developing mental toughness takes stumbling and falling on our faces sometimes but realizing that getting up is possible and carrying on is better. The human mind is powerful and can, through experience, develop the strength to overcome adversity. Mental toughness is like a muscle. It needs to be worked to grow and develop, and its strength is built up through small wins.

Firefighting requires courage and resilience, two major components of mental toughness. When the alarm sounds, I need to be ready, physically, and mentally. At a fire scene, I need to knock down one fire at a time, recalling habitual behaviors that have established a new norm in my brain that says, "You can do this."

Mental toughness means I can push the limits because I trust in myself and know I am prepared and ready to do what needs to be done. Each previous fire, extrication, or medical call has increased my mental strength to be able to handle each one that will come in the future. Fighting a **fully involved fire** will test my mental toughness and make me mentally tougher.

Advance or retreat, there is always a choice. We need to learn to listen to ourselves above the noise of others and build the daily habits that allow us to overcome distractions and break down challenges. Mental strength isn't about a dose of inspiration or courage; it's about habit and persistent movement toward our purpose. We build our mental toughness muscle, learning to believe in the power we have within ourselves to achieve our goals. Adversity will only make us stronger. We train our minds to resist the urge to quit, to be content with comfortable. We must know that if we show up, we will succeed.

"Mental strength is the ability to trust yourself in situations to know that it will be okay or that you need help."

Mental strength is the ability to trust ourselves in a situation to know that it will be okay and also to ask for help when we need it. Our life experiences give us mental strength if we learn from them. We need to believe in ourselves, to provide ourselves with the power to move forward. Unless we push the limits of our experiences, we can't gain our own trust. Trust in self is more challenging than trust in others and this trust is the basis of mental strength.

In 2012, I participated in the *Ironman Kona World Championship* race. I knew going into it that it would challenge me mentally and physically, but until I was wearing fifty pounds of firefighter gear walking down Queen Kamehameha Highway during the run portion and suffering the debilitating heat the Island delivers, I didn't fully understand the mental strength I would need. Not being a professional triathlete meant that I began the run portion after most of the professionals had finished the entire race.

I had been racing for over seven hours when I began the marathon. The heat from the lava field rocks was intense and I would endure an additional ten hours of racing, trying desperately to finish by midnight. The loneliness out on the road to the Energy Lab played with my mind, yelling at me to stop the insanity. I engaged in self-speak and let myself know that I could do this impossible task, that I was mentally stronger than the heat and loneliness.

As the night progressed, my exhaustion was real, and my suit was heavy. It wasn't known for its wicking qualities. There were pressure points from my sweat drying and rubbing. My feet generally swelled throughout the race and also took a beating from the weight. I weigh around 210 pounds on an average day, and with the gear, I am carrying about 260 pounds, not a usual triathlete weight. The helmet made me want to drop my head, but I had to look ahead to see where I was going. I think the tank was growing heavier too and my back hurt. I could usually handle the extra weight. As most triathletes know, it is the little irritations that cause the most problems, that challenge one's mental strength. For me, it is the water in my shoes, the rubbing of the gear and other things that bother me. I often have some raw spots on the hips and shoulders from the weight of the pack.

To keep going, I needed to be able to displace myself mentally from the race environment to a better place in my head.

The toughness of *Ironman* is legendary, but the toughness of the volunteers and spectators is equally a part of it. I drew on their energy to help me move forward. While I was not alone, it was up to me alone to decide that I could get it done. Under all the gear, within me, I summoned my trust in myself to keep going, one step at a time. I finished the race in 16:40.03, just short of the 17-hour deadline.

ACTION

List of why you Trust Yourself and who/what can help build you.

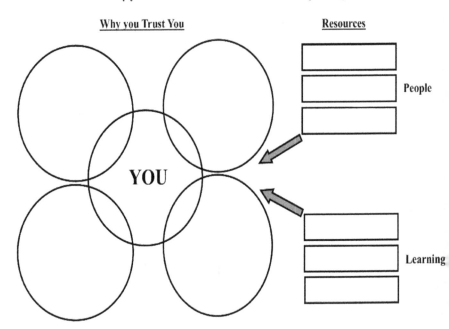

"You must be willing to suffer for success or be prepared to pay the price of regret."

Mental strength comes when we are challenged. To develop our mental strength, we have to be willing to suffer, not necessarily physically, but possibly emotionally. This powerful tool of mental strength in our lives can either debilitate us with regret and remorse for not having lived our dreams or build us up with fortitude to make the impossible possible. To discover our mental strength, we have to be willing to leave our comfort zone and endure the valleys on our way to the mountain peak.

I have a good friend, Bonner Paddock, who is an amazing person. He is the only person with cerebral palsy to summit Mount Kilimanjaro and finish the *Ironman World Championship* race. I met Bonner at that race in 2012. Bonner started a foundation, OM Foundation (One Man, One Mission), that builds rehabilitation facilities around the world to help disabled kids advance and feel empowered.

This mission for Bonner began in 2006 with a four-and-a-half-year-old boy named Jake, who also had cerebral palsy. Jake's dad, Steven, was participating in the Orange County Marathon as was Bonner. For the end of the race, Steven carried Jake across the finish line. Bonner had not known Jake or Steven before that day but bonded with them that day during the race. Then, Jake passed away in his sleep that night. This defining moment intensely changed Bonner's life, prompting him to create Team Jake.

In 2012, at Kona, Bonner and I had a conversation where Bonner asked, "Would you race for Team Jake sometime next year?"

"I'm in. Let's do this," I answered.

I picked *Ironman Lake Tahoe*, a first-year race. Not smart to do a first year, untested race, especially one with extreme elevation. But then, I knew I would have an angel on my side, pushing me up those mountains and pulling me along the run course -- little Jake.

The temperature at the swim's start was a balmy 38 degrees with overnight snow sparkling on the mountains. The water temperature was 60 degrees, but the swim went well. I exited the water to 40-degree temperatures. It was warming up, or not. My feet felt as if knives were cutting them as I ran to the changing tent. There was no room in the tent to change, so I did it outside, apathetic to what anyone might see. I was too cold to care.

Unable to stop shivering, I got on my bike, mentally preparing for the decreased oxygen of the Tahoe altitude. The bike course was crazy hard. After the first loop, I doubted whether I could finish or not. This was the 5th *Ironman* race of the year, and I was mentally and physically spent. On the second loop, before the big climb of close to 1,000 feet, I pulled into an aid station to call my wife ...for permission to stop. She didn't answer the two times I called. I kept going, anyway. My mental anguish and physical fatigue made me stop and walk the bike twice. I was talking and reasoning with myself, pushing through this part of the race to get to the transition to the run.

Out on the run, I continued to feel the pain from the 112-mile bike ride. Then, there was Bonner, who was not supposed to walk much after having done the race in Kona the previous year, walking beside me. I reassessed my motivation. I convinced myself that I had the strength to complete this race.

Two miles from the finish, I realized I had to run to finish within the 17-hour time. I ran in full gear (9:30/mile) after a long day, not because I was in great shape and my body was fresh, but because my mind told my body to do it with no excuses. Angel Jake pushed me, and I finished with 15 seconds to spare, then collapsed. I tempted fate with mind over matter and succeeded. It didn't feel that way at first.

ACTION

What is pain to you? Why would you be willing to go though it?

Define what pain means to you.

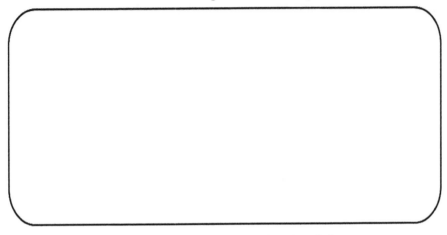

The Why you are willing to endure the pain for...

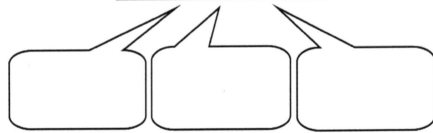

"Mental strength isn't about getting an incredible dose of inspiration or courage. It's about building the daily habits that allow you to overcome challenges and distractions over and over and over again."

Mental strength isn't about getting an incredible dose of inspiration or courage. It's about building the daily habits that allow us to overcome challenges and distractions over and over again. We don't become physically strong from lifting a barbell once or twice. We need to work overtime to develop physically as well as mentally in our strength. Every time we go through a situation that tests our mettle, a person's ability to cope with difficulties or a demanding situation. Whether we prevail or fail; we learn to boost our mental strength from merely having persevered. Our mental strength is borne of the other accelerants that work together over time.

I was offered an opportunity to be on a *Discovery Channel* reality show. The premise of the show was to put individuals who had lived through trauma and/or difficulties but were still dealing with the emotional fallout, into survival situations that would push their limits both physically and mentally. This would, in turn, help the individuals to create change in their lives. It was assumed that day-to-day life could not provide the impetus to make a permanent change. Only by stepping outside the box and experiencing a transformative ordeal could we approach this cathartic change to take ownership of something we had shoved away for years.

There were three of us, stranded on an island, JD, Sean, and I. It is firmly etched in my memory. We had a long day of foraging and getting everything set up for survival, such as the fire, shelter, and whatever we could find of food and water. We were seated beside the fire in the dark, talking about our lives, our experiences, and delving into deeply held emotions. I began to talk about my experiences during 9/11 and the impact it had had on my life. I then pulled out a tiny piece of the baby blanket that I had recovered on the last day of search and recovery. I had kept it and carried it with me from that point on, through all my triathlons, my time at the station, and always felt it was a symbol of why I was here. As I sat talking with my new brothers in survival around the fire, I realized something; I was carrying around my pain and calling it my purpose. It was then that I threw it in the fire. I was my purpose, alive, and with a heartbeat. I realized that life wasn't going to get any easier; I just needed to become stronger.

ACTION

What will you do daily to make building your potential a habit?

Traits of Mentally Strong people you know	Value to You	Daily habit to make yours
1.		
2.		
3.		
4.		
5.		
6.		
7.		

Chapter 10

FORGED
IN THE
FIRES

SUMMARY

**Hold on tight &
everything else will be alright.**

Chapter 10:

FORGED IN FIRE CONCLUSION

"Try not to become a person of success but a person of value. True Leadership begins with purpose and impacts through action."

It is about forging the best you in the fires of your life and coming out on the other side, mentally stronger to push your limits and create new ones. It is understanding that you are worth the pain and struggle, knowing that your passion will not be accepted by all and the path you may have to travel will be forged by you. Being forged in the fires is about turning your catalysts into daily habits that will help you lead yourself in the life you are meant to live.

ACTION

I, _____, commit to being the person I'm meant to be, even if I fall into darkness or challenges that seem too much. I will believe in me and remember my strength is in my passion. I am worth the time, struggle and journey to be the best me possible.

_____   _____
Signature   Date

I Survived
BECAUSE THE FIRE
INSIDE ME
BURNED BRIGHTER
THAN THE FIRE
AROUND ME.

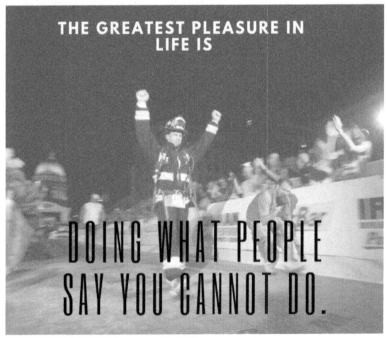

THE GREATEST PLEASURE IN
LIFE IS

DOING WHAT PEOPLE
SAY YOU CANNOT DO.

Chapter 11

Speaking / Consulting

Opportunity is not for those who want it...it is for those who go get it.

Chapter 11:

SPEAKING / CONSULTING

FIREMAN ROB VERHELST

Veteran Firefighter, Air Force Veteran, Reality TV Star.
September 11th Rescue Worker, & World Record Holder.
Bring In FIREMAN ROB to IGNITE your group.

FORGED IN THE FIRES
7 ACCELERANTS TO IGN

...YOUR MINDSET
...YOUR LIFE
...YOUR LEADERSHIP
...YOUR BUSINESS

WHY FIREMAN ROB IS THE IDEAL SPEAKER FOR YOUR EVEN

Robert "Fireman Rob" Verhelst is a dynamic storyteller with a unique, iconic story that brings your audience to
From numerous years in the fire service to surviving on Discovery Channel's show Ultimate Ninja Challeng
performing search and recovery after the September 11th attacks on the World Trade Center in New York
impact of his message resonates with everyone.

He continues inspiring the global community through his work as Fireman Rob, where he speaks, delivers trai
competes in Ironman races in 50 lbs. of firefighter gear, broke World Records, and delivers bears to childr
hospitals throughout the globe.

As an impact leader and in demand speaker/trainer, Fireman Rob impacts lives throughout the world throu
person events or his online training and social media presence. Robert truly lives and emphatically believes
there are no challenges or fears that cannot be overcome with the power of purpose and a strong mindset.
Our lives depend on strength to thrive, otherwise, we struggle to find success in life. It is the stories that con
Fireman Rob to the audience, allowing for a unique, genuine, and down-to-earth presentation. Driven by a d
to impact positive action in lives, "Fireman Rob" delivers an engaging presentation built on overcoming adve
validated under fire, and challenges each person to discover their purpose. His approach to purpose d
success pushes the uncomfortable, unknown limits of you and reveals simple, effective strategies that anyone
use to build mental strength, lead an "action based" lifestyle and become a better personal leader.

If you want to ignite the fires in your group or at your next event, Robert has the energy, experience and rec
message to make that happen. He is a normal guy with an extraordinary ability to push the envelope of wh
possible, and then relate it to others to do it in their own lives.

PARTIAL MEDIA LIST

Chapter 12

Additional Information

Chapter 12:

ADDITIONAL INFORMATION

In this chapter, I have included several articles written about me.

THE HOTTEST TRIATHLETE EVER

BY LINDSEY EMERY
OCT 25, 2012

Men's Health contributing author Lindsey Emery ventured to the 2012 Ironman World Championship in Kailua-Kona, Hawaii earlier this month to catch inspiring triathlete Robert Verhelst in action. Read on to see how he did—then watch him this Saturday at 4:00 p.m. ET on NBC.

It's almost 4:00 p.m. in Kona. The sun is shining, a soft breeze is in the air, and the temperature sits somewhere around 90 degrees. It's approximately nine hours and 12 minutes into the *Ironman World Championship*, and female pros Leanda Cave and Caroline Steffen are running their hearts out down Ali'i Drive, headed toward the finish line when we get the call.

"He's at transition. You've got about 8 minutes before he goes back out!"

We had just enough time to witness Cave win and Steffen come in a close second, rushing out minutes before Mirinda ("Rini") Carfrae would cross the line for third. The world's "hottest" Ironman—*literally*—was about to start his run, and we didn't want to miss it.

The transition zone is a sea of sleek carbon frame bikes. Everyone passing through quickly trades their aerodynamic helmets and cycling shoes in for wicking caps and running sneakers, hoping to shed some weight before they begin the grueling marathon portion of this race. Everyone but our guy, that is.

Rather than lighten his load for the long 26.2 miles ahead, 34-year-old Robert Verhelst puts on an additional 50 pounds of gear—a full firefighter's turnout kit, including an air tank and helmet—ties up his Newtons, and marches on to the course.

Because, you know, anyone can do an Ironman the "easy" way. And Verhelst (or Fireman Rob, as he's called), a firefighter, U.S. Air Force veteran and father of three from Madison, Wisconsin, isn't exactly one to take the easy way out.

"I Finally Feel Like Superman"

On September 13, 2001, just two days after the World Trade Center attacks, Verhelst drove to New York City and worked eight days straight, doing search, rescue, and recovery at Ground Zero. Ten years later, as a way to honor those who lost their lives on 9/11, the athletic fireman and recreational triathlete decided to do his first Ironman in Wisconsin on September 11, 2011, but instead of wearing shorts and a tank top like everyone else, he would tackle the run course in his turnout gear. No sweat. He also raised $8,000 for the Code 3 for a Cure Foundation, a non-profit that helps firefighters and their families who have been affected by cancer, in the process.

"You find strength in your passion," says Verhelst. "With the Ironman, I work my butt off all day like Clark Kent through the swim and the bike, and then I get to the run, and I finally feel like Superman, inspiring people to finish and hopefully reminding them of the sacrifices that others make every day."

This year, Verhelst's goal is to complete 10 full Ironman-distance races (2.4-mile swim, 112-mile bike, 26.2-mile run), sporting his firefighter's uniform for the marathon portion in each, and to raise $35,000 for Code 3 for a Cure. Kona was number eight on his list.

Fireman Rob is off, and he gets a much-needed boost from spectators along the run start. Pro Linsey Corbin stops en route to the finish, pats him on the shoulder and says, "You're amazing."

"The bike was brutal, it broke me down a lot, and I was distraught coming into transition. I knew what I had in front of me. I knew I had done it before, but I knew it was going to be a challenge," Verhelst says. "Then you get out there, you remember why you're doing it, you think about everyone who's relying on you, your friends, your family, and because it has a bigger meaning for you, you keep going."

Seven hours, 42 minutes and 13 seconds later, Ali'i Drive lights up with excitement, and Verhelst lands on the line, still suited up from head to toe, with a huge smile on his face. It's 11:40 p.m. -- 20 minutes before the race cut-off time—and he looks like the happiest guy in the world.

"A lot of people are very competitive, and that's great, but inevitably, we're not defined by what place we get. We're not defined by what time we get. We're not defined by how many races we do. We're defined by *how* we do the races," Verhelst says. "I'm going to go out there and give it everything I have, and at the end of the day, I'm proud of myself because I did it the way I knew was best."

The Rules of Fireman Rob

Want to beat the heat in your next big race? Follow Verhelst's training advice.

PREPARE FOR THE WORST

"I wear one of those garbage bag-suits and a 40-pound vest during my run workouts," says Verhelst. "It's extreme, but it helps prep me for what I'm about to face."

CHUG ON THE BIKE

The bike is the most crucial part of your hydration plan. "If you're already dehydrated by the time you get to your run, you're done," he says. During his ride, Rob drinks enough water to not get thirsty and takes an Endurolyte tablet about every hour, depending on the heat. He sips chicken broth (for the sodium) and water on his run.

REFUEL EARLY, REFUEL OFTEN

You lose calories like crazy on the course, so eat up while you can to prevent bonking. "I like fine dining when I'm on the bike, and since I'm from Wisconsin, which means I eat meat sticks (aka, beef jerky),"

Verhelst says. "I also love Nacho Cheese Combos and Cheese Nips Snack Mix."

STUFF YOUR SHORTS

Verhelst wears a wicking, long sleeve shirt and running tights under his uniform to prevent chafing. "On hot days, I have a cool towel around my neck and fill my pockets with ice at the aid stations," he says.

TALK TO YOURSELF

"Running in heat is about 80 percent mental, and you've got to talk yourself through to the finish," says Verhelst. "When I get to a hill, people will hear me say out loud, 'Get up that hill, get up that hill.' And at both turnarounds during Kona I was singing 'I'm Coming Home' in my head."

NBA.com

Bango and Bucks Bears Bring Smiles in Madison

Posted: Oct 20, 2015

Bango, the Bucks Dancers, the Fireman Rob Foundation visited the Ronald McDonald House and American Family Children's Hospital to deliver Bucks Bears to Madison area children before the Bucks preseason game at the Kohl Center.

Started in 2013, Robert "Fireman Rob" Verhelst created a Foundation that impacts the global community through a simple SMILE from a Bear. The foundation's mission is spreading the passion of being part of something bigger, one bear at a time, delivering smiles to children at hospitals throughout the world. Their 2015 Mission will include delivery of 2000 bears worldwide to children in hospitals and sending a deserving child, whose life has been affected by a trauma relating to burns, to Walt Disney World with our new Gift of Magic Project.

At the Bucks preseason game at the Kohl Center on October 20, The Fireman Rob Foundation and partners Southwest Airlines, Travel on a Dream & the Milwaukee Bucks, were honored to have a special young girl, Brooke Karper, and her family as honorary guests. When Brooke was 14 months old, she was trapped in a burning building where she sustained 60% burns to her body. She spent over 3 months in the hospital, going through grueling physical and occupational therapy to relearn how to use her hands, walk and speak again. Yet, no matter what Brooke has been through, she always has a smile on her face and a positive attitude. Thus, the Fireman Rob Foundation selected Brooke and her family to be special guests in launching the New Fireman Rob Foundation Gift of Magic Project. With amazing support from Travel on a Dream, Southwest Airlines & the Milwaukee Bucks, Brooke and her family are going to Walt Disney World.

The Iron Fireman
Tuesday, February 10, 2015 | By Brent Hannify

Rob Verhelst on service, family, and pushing your limits

Rob Verhelst had been a Wisconsin firefighter for less than a year when he watched the World Trade Center fall on live TV. 48 hours later, he'd packed up his car and driven to the city and spent eight days working alongside first responders at Ground Zero.

Rob has since forged himself into an inspiring figure for firefighters, first responders, endurance athletes, and the families who support them. Under the persona of Fireman Rob, he participates in IRONMAN and other triathlon races, finishing the final leg wearing 50 pounds of fireman's gear. A father of three and a philanthropist by nature, his current fundraising goal through the Fireman Rob Foundation is to deliver stuffed bears to children's hospitals around the world.

From the lava-scorched Kona fields to the brutal Utah switchbacks, spectators are intrigued and inspired by the sight of Fireman Rob, geared up in a full reflective Nomex jacket and 10-pound helmet, spreading his message of youth empowerment, philanthropy, and the pursuit of your passions with every mile.

Meet Fireman Rob in Part 1 of our blog series and come back for Part 2 when Rob gears up for his next IRONMAN in Oceanside, from the cool waters of the harbor to the challenging hills of Camp Pendleton.

Q&A

You were only 23 years old when you served at Ground Zero. Having spent less than a year in the fire service, how did that impact you?

I'd just got back from a house fire in Madison when I saw the second tower get hit. I didn't understand it. I felt displaced by it. But the same obligation which drove me to become a firefighter in the first place got me in the car the next day. I'd packed up my Saturn and started driving, since there were no flights in the air.

Because I was such a new firefighter, I admit I didn't have the experience that many of the veterans could rely on to handle a tragedy of this level. I worked to the best of my abilities, but it affected me for many years and still affects me today. But I have to be grateful for that opportunity to help, because it affected my life and made me who I am today.

What was the hardest race you've done so far, and what made it so tough?

One that stands out was the 2012 IRONMAN in St. George, Utah. I started swimming in Hurricane Lake, and I've got this glassy, still water that's keeping me moving. But then I realized why they named it that. I started to feel this chop, and I thought there was a boat next to me. But I looked up and saw no boat, just huge winds and four-foot waves. I had to decide, do I swim to the top of this wave, or duck under and pray to get a breath before the next one hits me? When I finally got out of the swim, I threw up twice, and staggered all the way through getting changed into my bike gear. I got through these brutal switchbacks, feeling seasick the whole time, and then when I was finally done I had about ten minutes to get into my fireman's gear before they closed the course for the day.

I started striding, but eventually the fatigue caught up with me. If you want an idea of what it felt like that day in the heat, put on three layers

136

of sweats and strap a ten-pound weight to your head. Now go walk around in 90-degree weather. I stopped and thought about quitting. But then people started coming up to me as I was catching my breath and they asked if they could go with me. Folks came up to me in flip flops, spectators just sitting on their lawns came up to me and gave me this energy. So, I started moving again. I rounded this one corner, and this mother and her son came up and she said she wanted her son to meet me. She said the boy's father, her husband, died of cancer, and that there were people out there doing things for them. That year I was doing the race for Code 3 for a Cure, which helps firefighters with cancer.

So, she and her son joined the crowd walking with me. I finished the race at 1 in the morning with a fire truck behind me, a police car in front, and about fifteen people along with my wife and my friends walking me to the finish line. That was the most impactful race finish I've ever had.

Any other memorable race moments that stand out?

Here's a great story. I was doing a tri over in Naples, FL, and I'm on my bike on this bumpy road and saw something you hardly ever see in Florida: A bald eagle. Seeing that bird made me so emotional, I started belting out Lee Greenwood's "God Bless the USA." Just me on my bike with no one around, a bald eagle flying overhead, and I'm singing out loud *"... and I'm proud to be an American, where at least I know I'm freeee ...."*

That got me through the next ten miles.

Aside from your fireman's gear, what are some other things you carry during your races?

Well, I don't wear boots. I wear running shoes. They're more practical and comfortable. Also, underneath the fire gear, I wear compression tech shirts and leggings because Nomex chafes like crazy if you don't have anything underneath it.

137

On a personal note, I also keep something I found in the rubble at Ground Zero: One night, I was walking off The Pile and saw a baby blanket. I went down and pulled it up and brought it home. I had it made into a blanket that my son now sleeps with every night, and I keep a piece with me in my fire jacket every time I race. I carry it because, while I'm realizing my passion, I remind myself that there are a lot of people who didn't get the chance to realize theirs. I carry it for them.

How many more races do you think you've got left?

All I know is I love going out there and being a positive influencer. I've seen other guys in fire gear, and I've seen guys in military fatigues running those races. My life doesn't have a preset path. I love going out where my life takes me, and I'll do this as long as I possibly can. If I can, I'll still be out there at age 90 in full gear at Kona. That'll be an interesting day, but I'm going to do it.

What advice would you give to someone who wants to get into firefighting?

You have to ask yourself, "Do I have a passion for service? Do I care about the safety of my community?" When you go to work as a firefighter, you are giving yourself to your community every day. It's not just about doing the job, it's about the passion for it. Talk to other firefighters. Understand what the mission is. If your heart and your body are in it, go forth.

I remember one structure fire early in my career; we were first on the scene at about 2:00 in the morning. The fire had already blown out every window and was venting through the roof and we stacked up at the door. Right before we went in, I had this moment where I realized I was putting my trust in my fellow firefighters. It's about brotherhood.

I think that's a huge aspect of what's developed my character. You just instinctually do, and you trust and rely on the people who support you.

The people in the fire station I work with, and the people who visit GovX ... they all chose to serve and protect. If we can be passionate about this service, we can bring that to our communities, and this idea of service and positive influencing will spread. There's a sense of healing, belonging, and solace that comes from helping our communities, and I see it every day.

There are no shortcuts to any place worth going

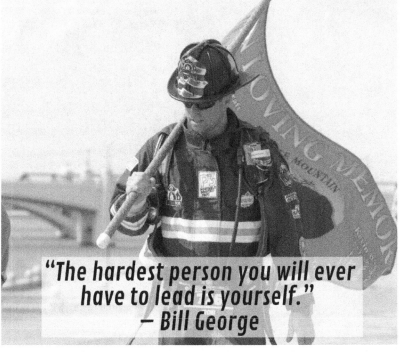

"The hardest person you will ever have to lead is yourself."
— Bill George

Don't count the days, make the days count.

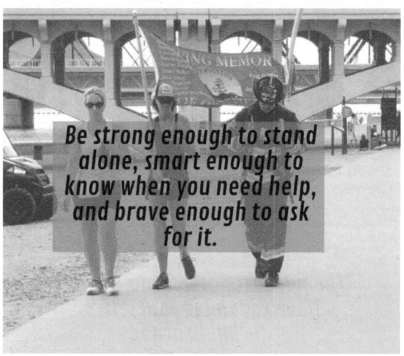

Be strong enough to stand alone, smart enough to know when you need help, and brave enough to ask for it.

CONTACT THE AUTHOR

Thank you for reading my book. I have one favor to ask. Will you please leave an honest review on Amazon for me? I would really appreciate it. Also, reach out to and let me know what you think. I can be contacted at Robert@VSuccessNetwork.com by email or through my website at www.FiremanRob.com.

MY FOUNDATION WEBSITE

www.FiremanRobFoundation.com

Made in the USA
Las Vegas, NV
15 May 2021

23117022R00089